for Jocelyn

Jon.

So, Let Me Just Say

So,
Let Me
Just Say

Jon Adams

Xulon Press

Xulon Press
2301 Lucien Way #415
Maitland, FL 32751
407.339.4217
www.xulonpress.com

Scripture quotations taken from the King James Version
(KJV) – *public domain.*

Scripture quotations taken from the New English Bible (NEB).
Copyright ©1970 by Oxford University Press and Cambridge
University Press.Used by permission. All rights reserved.

Printed in the United States of America.

ISBN-13: 9781545621813

For Rachel and Stephanie

Table of Contents

Who am I.......and even more troubling, Who are you?

An Introductory Essay

I first thought about joining the poetry and the biography together in one book, one following the other. However, the more I thought about this the more I thought that this placement was unattractive. Moreover, the content of each seems so very different. Was the person who wrote the biography the same person who wrote the poetry? Could the same person be seen in both or did they express significantly different personalities? It seemed, to me at least, that these were not ridiculous questions. In the end I decided not to include the complete collection of poetry. Yet the question remains.

What Is a Good Person? Are Any of Us Good?

The human personality is made up of beliefs, values, experiences, preferences, knowledge, habits etc. that often have no real connection to each other. Vladimir Putin, the President of Russia, may be an egotistical tyrant but apparently he is a great fan of the Beatles, and especially likes the song "Yesterday". What connection has one thing with the other? Almost certainly nothing. One could spend a delightful evening with him listening to the Beatles, but would one feel as comfortable if he was expressing other less innocent ambitions and preferences?

Can a person, for example, be described as good if they possess six good characteristics, and yet have four evil aspects, or contrariwise, six evil characteristics and four exceptionally praiseworthy ones? So what is it that defines a person? Can just one aspect of an individual be taken as a defining characteristic, one that potentially negates all others? How is it possible to have one or more admirable qualities, and yet simultaneously possess one or several evil qualities? Or is this way of looking at an individual completely wrong? Indeed, is this "accountant" methodology of evaluating a person, God's way?

I suspect that most of us divide the human race, from a moral point of view, into three categories: the exceptionally good (saints), the neither very good nor very bad, or in other words, the "decent" (most of the human race), and the very evil (criminals and tyrants). This taxonomy, however, can have no real objectivity, no real aspect as fact, as it appears to express only the point of view of the middle group, which generally subscribes to this categorization.

In addition, the middle group, in comparing itself to the other two extreme groups, tends *not* to take its weaknesses and failures very seriously and sees itself as belonging more to the "saints" than to the "evil" group, defining itself as "decent". Furthermore, a different perception could well be arrived at if one were in either of the other two groups.

God's Description of a Person Who is not Good

Moreover, God represents a fourth "group" and definitely appears to view things from an entirely different perspective. And this is that *all* have sinned and fallen short of God's essential nature, that there is none that does good, no not one. In other words, one is not good if one could do, would do, or does even a single act of evil. Consequently, if it takes just one sin to alienate oneself from God there is no such thing as mortal and venial sins, all sins are mortal. Both of these previous evaluations of human beings are scriptural statements. So from God's perspective, *at least at one initial point in time in each individual's life,* there is only one kind of human being, and that is that *each person* is sinful and unacceptable to God.

In fact, God's view of personal goodness is shockingly antithetical to ours. The tiny book of James in the New Testament chapter 2 verse 10 states, "For if a man keeps the whole law apart from one single point, he is guilty of breaking all of it." Luke 6:43-45 does not improve this disturbing position. God's starting point, though not (his) end point, is that we are all failures. Not a very pleasant perception, don't you agree?

If that is so, then *no one* should view themselves as morally superior to any other human being. This is not an easy proposition for most people to accept. Having spent our entire lives judging/evaluating ourselves, even if unconsciously, in comparison to other human beings, such a proposition, such a position, if we are honest, seems not only inaccurate but ridiculous.

At the best, the God view is seen as acceptable only from a religious point of view, but existentially and practically irrelevant. This however is actually a rejection of the God view for it interprets such a view as simply an idea, as opposed to an objective fact, that is, it does not express the reality of the situation.

And what is perhaps more surprising, is that many, if not most Christians, deep in their hearts, would support this position. To say that most people are essentially decent and good, while simultaneously believing that "all have sinned and fallen short of the glory of God" (Romans 3:23) is an internal contradiction that radically minimizes God's evaluation of the human race. After all, how can one say within oneself, "I am a sinner but I am essentially good"? Is God overstating his case?

There are some people, on the other hand, who regard themselves as morally inferior to other human beings. This group is deeply conscious of behavioural and moral/religious failure, but at various times, it includes most people in the middle group, for who is not conscious of at least occasional failure? For many, this becomes a little dance in which they take differing positions on the issue, depending on whom they are comparing themselves to. Nevertheless, if we take the God view at all seriously, even those we regard as morally superior to us must not be seen as superior, *in themselves*.

Now it is admittedly obvious that there are some people who, in some sense, are better, more decent than other people. Abraham Lincoln was an incredibly forgiving and quite gentle person, and I am sure that St. Francis, for example, realized he was "better" than most of the people around him. But apart from the fact that, in his case, he would not have thought this a reason for pride or superiority, scripture teaches that before the experience of faith in the work of Christ, all have failed to meet God's standard of moral and spiritual perfection, and essentially, this is the theme of the first seven chapters of the Pauline book of Romans.

This must be the situation, for if there is no one who expresses the character of God, as stated above, then anyone who does express God's character must have achieved this from a source outside themselves, and therefore can have no reason to feel superior. This source, if one takes a biblical standpoint, is God (Him)self. Yet, while one may rejoice in whatever level of holiness one has achieved, in the truest sense, one has achieved any level of true holiness only as a result of the work of the Holy Spirit transforming the heart into the nature of God.

Yet, not taking the God view seriously, as most of the human race, including the religious, do, makes the God view an extremely difficult position to defend, not only intellectually but also psychologically, as most of the human race has spent all or most of their lives with an entirely different viewpoint.

Can a Person Become Good Without God?

Furthermore, forgetting God for the moment, the "position on a gradient" theory completely ignores why and how someone *becomes* either more or less "good". Clearly, where one was born, who one's parents were, the social class one was born into, one's economic state, the psychological environment one finds oneself in, indeed the historical period in which one was born, all determine, if there are no other contrary inputs, the moral person one will eventually become.

If Adolph Hitler had been born into an Amish family in Pennsylvania, is it at all likely that he would have turned into the kind of person he inevitably did become?

Indeed, the moral state of an individual appears to be predominantly the result of pure chance, (unless one believes there is no such thing as, for want of a better word, chance, which, from one perspective, necessarily makes God the author of evil) and while one's moral state is crucial and has definite objective impacts, human vulnerability to external forces/variables makes our evaluation of both the person and such results, highly suspect and troubling.

Can a Person Change Their Personality?

In addition, to this mix must be added the possibility of alteration in one's personality, which is, in fact, the corollary of the idea that one's moral state is predominantly formed after one's birth. One is not born with either a good or evil moral nature. Perhaps one should say that human beings are born with a vulnerable/susceptible nature.

A refusal to accept that an individual can alter his/her personality has been, I suspect, a deeply rooted belief throughout history, based primarily on ignorance and fear. In addition, there exists in many, if not most within the population, an internally contradictory belief that while some people can change, certain other kinds of people cannot. Put absolutely simplistically, what this boils down to is, "someone like me can change but others who are significantly unlike me, cannot".

The belief in the total inability of some individuals to change, frequently depends on the degree of societal rejection of certain characteristics, and fear of, and repulsion towards the people seen to possess such characteristics. Over history, the group that has incited such social loathing and intransigence has been transferred from one set of people to another, for example, witches, communists and homosexuals, each one, at different times in history, exerting a seemingly unstoppable and "incontrovertible" passion in the society, in that passionate opposition to these "socially destructive" groups was believed to be supported by incontrovertible "facts".

And while over time these views and passions have been dropped and completely or partially rejected by later societies, this occurs, unhappily, not before hundreds, if not thousands have suffered, sometimes terribly, in these mistaken beliefs.

My own sense of horror at this does not come from the realization that society has been tragically mistaken as to these various groups, but from the apparent human willingness, indeed at times passionate willingness and desire to inflict sometimes excruciating pain, humiliation, torture and even death on other human beings because they are different.

Given that the majority of the population is made up of what I have termed the "decent" people, classifying individuals as fixedly evil, often the conclusion of an elite within this majority, seems to be that a certain characteristic, felt to be socially repulsive, and even sinful, permanently characterizes the individual guilty of such socially unacceptable acts.

Consequently, these decent individuals find it inconceivable that these "non-decent" others who have chosen to locate themselves within the extremely evil third group, and who have performed such acts, can ever be trusted to never again repeat such behaviour, in fact, that the unacceptable behaviour is an intrinsic part of their nature.

Our Difficulty To Accept That a Person Has Changed

Indeed, while the decent people are never described by any of the acts which they perform, as if these acts do not permanently describe their personalities, the non-conforming individuals are often permanently branded by the act which separated them from the middle group of society, and suffer for years after the event, despite never having engaged in such act(s) since.

So not only do we need to include environmental variables in our understanding of the human personality, we need to include a dynamic understanding of the process of behavioural change, as a result of various kinds of new data inputs that affect the nature of an individual, and that can effect change in an individual.

Personal Responsibility and How It Is Used to Justify Guilt and Punishment

It is, on the other hand, necessarily true that each person is responsible for his/her actions. After all, one's actions are not performed by an entirely other person. Further, it is of great import that an individual realize not only *why* an action was done but also that it was done by them. Simply understanding why an action was done does not exculpate the person, nor does it remove the objective ownership of the act or its result(s) as this impacts on another person and the world.

Yet individual responsibility can, and definitely must not be the only criterion on which an individual is evaluated. Those variables also, which are entirely psychological variables, which explain why an individual acts, must be taken seriously, *by the observing other.* And at varying times we all are the observing other.

Individual good/evil must be seen, therefore, from the aspect of point of view. That is, the points of view of the individual him or herself, and that of an observing other.

Our Difficulty to Take the Psychological Causes of Another's Personality Seriously

It may be argued that we can never completely know the reasons, the personal history that cause an individual to act as they do, and therefore we can never observe another person with sufficient knowledge to evaluate their behaviour, but this is an empty argument. It is enough to know that for the acting individual there were compelling reasons that, for them, were strong enough to cause the person to act as they did, even if, objectively, these reasons were incorrect and even destructive. And furthermore, this paradigm of decision-making is identical for each and every one of us, no matter the content of the decision in question.

This must necessarily be true, not only for those guilty/ responsible for small wrongs, but also and more importantly for those guilty of more serious wrongs. What should follow from this is not necessarily an emptying of all jails but can be *nothing less than a radical rethinking of ways we deal with and view those responsible for extreme wrongs.*

Taking the psychological (not necessarily in the sense of a psychopathology) seriously, involves an inner dialectic/conversation one has with oneself, and is often experienced as a conflict, a struggle *against* the evaluation of the acts and person, along the lines of the internalized positions and conclusions of one's society that one possesses, virtually against one's will and of which one is frequently unaware, as a member of one's society. In a sense, one struggles against the ideas and feelings of one's socialized self.

This taking of such variables seriously by the observing other *needs* however, to be done, not solely for the sake of truth, but also from the point of view of self-interest. There is, after all, not one person on this planet who is not, at various *times, both the* perpetrator of unacceptable acts, and the one being evaluated.

A Spiritual Incentive to Refrain From Judging Others

But I will add one more reason why these psychological variables must be taken into consideration, and why intellectual compassion (that is, compassion based on reason) is not anti-thetical to justice and truth. There is not one person, not one, not you and certainly not me, who will escape God's rigorous, complete, absolute, and total examination and evaluation. This will be done with a compassion and divine love that in many cases will have been absent from much of our own trivial evaluation of other sinful human beings, who have, on the contrary, experienced only the hardness of our hearts and the lack of true forgiveness that are sadly so much a part of our being.

Moreover, this discovery of our true evil will be accompanied by an ever increasing horror and shame, and sense of guilt that will come as a result of God's revelation to us of the sinfulness, and self centeredness that have permeated each of our lives. Indeed, this sinfulness in its commonality, its social ordinariness, will be shown to have become so much a part of our nature and the nature of those around us, that we have become inured, blind to its overwhelming horror, and unaware that it is the core of our nature, our default position when under stress.

I have experienced a little of what this means, but I am sure that much horror at the sinfulness of my life awaits me when I finally meet God after my death. Thankfully, God will heal my heart and your heart too. God will indeed wipe away every tear, both for the unhappiness and terrible sorrow of our lives and also resulting from and because of the unbearable, overwhelming and inescapable shame and guilt we will finally feel, at what we discover, but discover this we will.

Perhaps the Most Surprising Discovery We Will Make After We Die

With this, that sense of our human decency and goodness, that has allowed us to look our neighbour in the eye without shame and fear, will be discovered to be the filthy rags the scripture has said it is, even though, at present, we do not truly believe this. Nor are "unbelievers" the only ones with this belief in their own decency. Deep in the heart of many, maybe most Christians is the feeling that they are decent people, in complete contradiction to Isaiah 64:6. And this is, at least part of the reason we should take Matthew 7: 3-5 seriously.

All Those We Regard As Sinners

Sinners, understood in a secular sense, include all who, to one degree or another, act in ways which we do not accept. Human beings are extremely judgemental, and evaluate the words and actions of virtually every person or group met, read about and interacted with every day of their lives, rejecting and reacting to almost every behaviour or statement indicating a difference. Jesus was extremely interested in the way we look at (other) sinners, and maybe even more so, in the way we treat them.

Repentance: Its Necessity and Consequences

In religious terms, repentance, which involves an epiphanic understanding of previously held self-destructive attitudes and behaviours, and results in a turning away from such behaviours and attitudes, (often, but not always in conjunction with the new birth) is the result of an infusion of new data that can potentially and radically alter an individual's personality. Not incidentally, repentance implies, on God's part, that, *as all are commanded to repent, all unacceptable behaviour can be altered.*

Free Will and the Cutting of the Gordian Knot of Responsibility

The concept of "free will" appears to cut the Gordian knot in our understanding of personal responsibility, but, in essence, free will negates and ignores all the aspects of environment, and indeed "nature", if one includes aspects of character that we appear to be born with that do actually impact the developing human personality.

Two Weaknesses in Our Understanding of Free Will

Free will assumes that we could have chosen to act in an entirely different fashion, *for if one could not have acted in an alternate fashion, one would necessarily not be free.* And it must be admitted that there frequently do exist alternative possibilities, some real some theoretical, to any chosen behaviour. The fact remains, however, that to accept free will is to minimize or deny the absolute importance of environment, and completely fails to answer the question of *why* one behaviour is chosen over another.

Moreover, in its outworking it implies an essential human nature that apparently, intuitively knows right from wrong, and even more so, presumably also intuitively knows the optimal way to act in virtually every situation, whereas human experience and history clearly show that such understandings/ decisions/choices are highly culturally, psychologically, and historically determined.

A prime example of this is the current social repulsion to stories and videos of beheadings by IS soldiers. It is not many centuries ago that such events, burnings at the stake, the barbarity of state ordered hanging, drawing and quartering of treasonous offenders, and other horrors were an accepted part of our own society. One suspects that social punitive behaviours that we take as acceptable will also, in time, be viewed with a similar horror.

Systems of Ethics and How We Acquire Them

Even if, for a moment, one were to accept free will as an existent, is a knowledge of right and wrong inherent? Who teaches an individual right and wrong? Which society's or culture's sense of right and wrong is correct? Indeed are any cultural systems of ethics correct? And if one's system of right and wrong is not inherent, then one's moral decisions are based upon a multiplicity of varying systems of formally and informally taught ethics, and free will is not a particularly useful tool to explain such behaviour.

Free Will As Empty Tautological Thinking

For what is the value of free will if it does not have the potential to result in optimal choices? And if optimal choices are not the expected result then there must have been a choice arrived at from the individual's internally and probably inadequately held beliefs and knowledge. And if this is the case, then what is the point in assigning free will such importance as the explanation of chosen behaviours and as the source of decisional responsibility? It is simply tautological, surely along the lines of "something was chosen because it was chosen", thus explaining nothing. Free will is, after all, a utilitarian belief.

Perhaps this is an appeal to an extrinsic value, and not to the/an intrinsic understanding of what free will is, but if the understanding of the concept ignores both the objective variables that are the true basis of all decision making, and ignores also the use/misuse of the concept in its outworking, surely the concept has been shown to be essentially vacuous, untrue and operationally of little use, invalid in the common understanding of the word.

Free Will as the Ignoring of the Psychology of Choice, and the Assertions of One's Beliefs

Moreover, in answer to this seemingly nonsensical reasoning, that does not know where to accurately place the responsibility for choice, how we actually do choose is based upon the usually limited and often inadequate information we have, that we take to be knowledge, and that we take to be accurate representations of the external world. And if this is the case, no choice is free as the choices are determined by the often complex internally held sets of data that are actually held to be true.

It must also be noted that an individual's asserted comments on what they believe to be true cannot necessarily be held to be what they actually believe. These personal assertions are not expressions of dissimulation, but rather instances of what the individual believes should be true or has been taught is true, as opposed to what the person actually believes is true. Though it often takes a crisis to determine what that actually is.

Erroneous Beliefs Regarding the Evaluation of Another's Decisions

Furthermore, it is of absolutely no account that these individually held beliefs, that are taken as knowledge, are frequently untrue. It is equally unimportant, or problematic that the observing other believes his/her beliefs to be accurate, or at least more accurate understandings of reality, and that they must in their turn therefore have been as equally understood, obvious and accepted by the doer of the act, prior to the doing of the act.

Judgement and the Power to Enforce Such Judgements

That the perpetrator and observer may, and frequently do possess (two) quite differing views of the world is almost always *not* taken into consideration by either party, but with the one possessing greater power able to control the outcome of the conflict.

The Nuremberg war crimes trials immediately come to mind in this, where the defendants' appeal to the necessity of following the chain of command appears to accept the very claim that the prosecutors were making that the men accused had knowingly violated basic and accepted humane moral positions on the slaughter of defenceless human beings, moral positions, the prosecution asserted, that the accused themselves held. Yet the assumption that these values were in fact shared was the very point that should have been questioned. The accused, thus, were implicitly admitting their guilt.

Moreover, it is relatively simple to show that in the vast panoply of genocidal behaviour that was performed, many actions by the Nazis and the military were willingly carried out and were not the result of command coercion.

On the other hand, the prosecution's rejection of the chain of command necessity was an act of pure hypocrisy, as no military and para-military organization in the world would accept the right of any of its members to make a moral decision in regard to command decisions such that it would allow members not to carry out an order. Nevertheless, global horror at this genocidal barbarity and cruelty was totally justified.

The Illogic of Free Will in the Evaluation of Another's Choices

If choosing is the "doing of," or "coming down on" one option and not another, then the "choosing" of one option is either *inevitably based on the "weight" of one option over the other(s), or human choice is totally irrational and not based on any of the sets of internally available data.* That we choose is obvious, that we choose freely is less so.

Indeed, the concept of free choice seems to depend on a choice that appears to be determined by no actually held inherent values and psychological positions. In this scenario human beings make irrational and frequently unpredictable choices that, in some cases, are assumed to violate the actor's own set of held values.

Ascribing irrationality, moreover, to another's choices is the "irrational" imposition of the observer's own perception of reality onto that of the 'acting' other. And quite possibly both perceptions of rationality vis-a-vis the act being evaluated may be incorrect. Free will is thus posited as the explanation of such unpredictable and irrational behaviour with and in much the same pseudo-explanatory manner and vigor that medieval cosmology asserted the nature of the visible and invisible cosmos with the earth at its centre.

Indeed, belief in the apparent obviousness of free will is remarkably similar to the long held belief in the earth as the centre of the solar system. These both seem to be necessarily true because they appear so obvious to our experience. Yet, if one is now universally accepted as incorrect, why should we believe the other is necessarily correct?

Furthermore, if there *are* inherent reasons why someone acts as they do, (though they are at variance with those values held by an observer or observers, and even with the stated beliefs of the actor) it cannot be said that the choice is free, for the choice is determined by pre-existing complexes of value and knowledge. That we appear to act freely is readily admitted, but that we actually act freely can only be illogical.

Moreover, given that most cognitive activity goes on at the subconscious level, the conscious mind is usually not aware of most decisional processes going on at this subconscious level, and so the individual may not even realize why they have made the decisions they subsequently make. In addition, given the felt need sometimes to explain decisions made, the explanations provided may be only partly accurate, or even completely incorrect or inadequate, drawing, as they do, from data that exists predominantly from the level of consciousness and may, in fact, contain values and beliefs that are the products of socialization, but not held at the subconscious level.

Two Grounds on Which Free Will Fails

Free will fails on two grounds. It fails because, though it may admit that there are inner values and knowledge, these do not necessarily determine the direction of the choice because the actor, somehow, paradoxically, could have chosen to act based (apparently) on values and knowledge frequently not possessed by the actor, and such a possibility is both illogical and impossible. Further, it fails in that if there are no values and knowledge that determine a choice, the choice is made based upon no determining factors, that is, for no apparent reason, and that also is impossible to believe. And moreover, this lack of determining factors vitiates any attempt to impute *responsibility and blame to the* actor/decision maker.

The Noble Intent Behind Free Will

Free will seeks to elevate the human to the nobility of a free soul, a twin to the equally non-sensical term *homo sapiens,* the self congratulatory term our species has given itself, and by implication denying this quality to other hominid groups, let alone other life forms that possess intelligence and creativity. However, the de facto result is only to reduce humanity to the ridiculous source of decisions based on nothing firm, simply because there frequently *appears* to exist the possibility of an alternative, more "reasonable" choice.

For, as those who would support the idea of free will must assert, if there is only one possible choice, there is no freedom. The binary possibility that there always exists an alternative choice, that is *a* and *not a,* cannot be used to assert that in the real world either of these possibilities is always existentially a possibility.

Are We Robots? Does a Rejection of Free Will Imply a Radical Determinism?

This overall conclusion, however, has historically been seen as problematic in terms of what it means to be human. Human beings are presumably not controlled by some external entity. If, however, individuals are not free to choose contrary to what is consciously and sub-consciously held to be true, then in what sense do humans make free choices? The most reasonable conclusion is that they do not, and I would suggest that the problem we find in this exists because of and within the concept of free choice itself.

A Different Understanding of the Self That Asserts a View of the Self As the Active Agent of Choice

Perhaps we need to abandon the entire concept of freedom of choice and construct a new and different understanding that accepts limitation, while not concluding that we are robots. Perhaps part of the solution to this is to posit that there is a living being, (itself a mysterious entity) who is able to make dynamic decisions, conclusions based upon what is held to be true, and in an optimal situation, where what is held to be true is actually so. It may well be that the rapid development of AI will one day force us to find an answer to this question.

In rejecting free will as the explanation for decision making and suggesting that all decisions are the result of internally held complexes of data received over a lifetime, I am not suggesting that, as humans we are programmed or controlled in any way other than in relation to data held to be true. Rather, this living being possesses a decision making ability which involves choosing outcomes and conclusions based on the information and data (correct and erroneous) that the mind has accumulated. These conclusions, and the clusters of related conclusions are the lenses through which the world and what happens in it are interpreted.

The total body of data accumulated during one's lifetime does not equal, and cannot be identified with the self, the dynamic being who interacts with this data. That there is usually a consequence, a product, a set of intellectual conclusions that influence and determine behaviour resulting from an interpretation of this data, a kind of reaction to the data, indicates or at least suggests, the existence of a separate self which interacts with this data. There is in this, a fluidity, a dynamism to choice that is entirely non-robotic, not coerced. Decision-making is, thus, the mind of the individual actively choosing a conclusion in each situation.

This choosing experience may, it is acknowledged, be affected or even limited by the efficiency of the brain one possesses to internally communicate the data to the self for interpretation, but it is based solely on the data that resides in the brain/mind.

What we have then is actually an understanding of the acts of will that is based on a more objective, more scientific model of decision making. Indeed, what we have is a personality which makes choices, usually unconscious/subconscious, based upon the information it possesses, that it concludes is objective data, but which, once again, may, in fact, not be. We have thus a limiting set of data which is the pool from which the dynamic personality makes decisions and arrives at conclusions. There is true decision making going on that is neither a robotic, mechanical operation that denies human input nor an irrational choice devoid of intellectual content. Rather, it is a genuine, dynamic (if far from simple) process resulting in a genuine choice.

The Rejection of Free Will As a process of Decision Making, Not Even Possessed by God

Free will is a chimera, at the best an illogical concept, at the worst an excuse both personal and societal, for revenge, hatred and devaluation. Not even God has perfect freedom to choose, or do we believe that God could choose to be evil?

The Necessity to Reject Our Moral Superiority

Further, to return to the initial question of who we are in the deepest parts of our being, I believe that before we can accept another person as they truly are we must have a deep understanding of who we ourselves are, and have come to forgive, and in a sense accept, the "unacceptable" in ourselves. Indeed, to accept God's forgiveness of one's sins implies (more than suggests) that one should forgive oneself, for if God has forgiven one one's sin, and no longer takes it/them into account, what right have we to continue to act as if this is not so? Those who cannot, or refuse to admit the unacceptable in themselves will certainly not accept the wrongs in others.

Indeed, what other possible meaning can be derived from Jesus' words in the Gospel of Matthew 7: 3-5, where he states,

> Why do you behold the mote (splinter) that is in your brother's eye but ignore the beam (great log) that is in your own eye? Or how will you say to your brother, 'let me pull the mote out of your eye', and look, a beam is in your own eye? You hypocrite, first cast the log out of your own eye and then you shall see clearly how to cast out the splinter from your brother's eye."

Incidentally, the implication here seems to be that we *all* have "great logs", faults, sins, wrongs, mistakes in ourselves, and only when we realize this, can we deal with, evaluate, react to the wrongs in others. This is the most common interpretation of this parable.

However, it should also be noted that Jesus does not say, "take the splinter out of your own eye and then you shall see clearly". Perhaps the beam in our eyes is not a fault or particular wrong at all, but rather some *particular character lack we* have that makes it impossible to view the wrongs of others correctly.

But if the beam reveals what we lack, what is it that we do have? So what is the beam? And, moreover, comparing the size of what "exists" in our eyes, what we have "in our eyes" is of greater significance and *detriment to the evaluation of "the other" than* the "splinter" that exists in the lives of those we are finding at fault. Perhaps what we lack is the nature/the mind of God, and I will not suggest what that is, other than point to the character of Jesus.

God's Seemingly Ridiculous Mathematics

With that in mind it seems appropriate to return for a moment to the verse in the book of James that appears to be mathematically unthinkable. So if one obeys all the hundreds of commands in the Law of Moses but fails to obey just one law, that person is guilty of breaking the Law. This statement in James does not seem to be fair at all. Doesn't God know what it means to be human?

This, however, is not the way to look at the verse.

The Two Ways We Become Human

There are two ways human beings acquire their personality, their character. The first is the way described in this introduction: through an accumulation of data, begun almost certainly in the womb and continued as long as we live and experience the world and other human beings. This method/experience is fraught with danger, error, and frequently, psychological pain, and ends in one being suffused with varying levels of distrust and dislike of other human beings.

The fact that there are no consistent, uniform patterns of data accumulation means that each person is psychologically distinct from every other person and consequently views the world, to a greater or lesser degree, differently to every other person.

If we are lucky we have a vision/idea of how human beings should act harmoniously towards each other, however our struggle to achieve this vision inevitably encounters all those aspects of our personality that are contrary to this vision.

Given the positive and negative inputs that have created the person we are, whatever degree of goodness we do achieve does not arise as an expression of an inherent natural goodness, but is the result of a fortunate environment and inner struggles to rise above our failings, repeated acts of determination, and socialization. In other words, goodness does not spring naturally from our hearts but from our will, our intellect and choices not to do evil, despite our desire to do just that.

What James Was Attempting to Show Us

What James, chapter 2 is attempting to show us is that if we sin, even once, this is evidence that our hearts are not naturally good and holy. Whether one believes the Adamic fall of man story in Genesis or not, the Fall was generated, according to this story by only one sin which was *essentially symbolic, as* Adam's sin was rebellion against God, not the eating of a piece of fruit. This "one sin" in James is similarly symbolic and primarily the *symptom* of our dilemma, not the mathematical number that alienates us from God. We sin, therefore, because we do not *inherently* possess a holy nature, (and holiness is simply the nature of God).

Probably everything in the universe acts as its nature determines. And if one wishes to claim that violence, distrust, anger and a lack of universal love *are* intrinsic expressions of human nature, clearly human beings are not naturally good.

This is not to say, however, that we do not long to be good. The human problem is *not solely in what* we do, so much as it is the inefficient, "accidental" and ineffective way we acquire our personalities.

The Seemingly Ludicrous Other Way

Yet, though we do not, acquire an inherently "good" nature at birth, the purpose of the "new birth", alluded to in the Gospel of John, is to do just that.

Are Christians No Different to Non-Christians?

All other human beings are brothers and sisters as fellow human beings, all others are our neighbours, (the parable of the Good Samaritan shows us that) our behaviour to all others, Christian and non-Christian should be the same, motivated by love, yet all people are not the same. Christians are simply human beings, in themselves they are sinners, as are all others, have similar needs to all others on the planet, and share similar fears and longings, yet Christians are different. This allows Christians no reason to feel superior. This difference also has nothing to do with superior religious doctrine, nothing to do with race, and absolutely nothing to do with personal qualities, intellect or praiseworthy moral character.

Moreover, one must put aside any understanding one may have on the wrath of God towards sinners, for the wrath of God, however this is understood, or even rejected, has nothing to do with the difference between Christians and non-Christians.

Wherein Then Does This Difference Lie?

The difference is solely found in that when one experiences the new birth, the Holy Spirit, the Spirit of Jesus, enters the heart and soul of the human and begins the process of writing the law of God (God's holy nature) on the heart of an individual so that godliness gradually becomes the *nature* of the person.

Salvation Is Not Simply a Matter of Forgiveness

Salvation is at least a twofold process. The first is becoming a child of God. The new birth is where the forgiveness of sin (Jesus' work on the cross) becomes ours, the Righteousness of Christ is given to us, where, metaphorically speaking, we are clothed in the robe/covering of his righteousness and we become Righteous in Him. This is not simply a legal ascription. It involves an existential change in our being, as in the words of St. Paul, "if anyone is in Christ they are a new being, old things are passed away and all things have become new." It is the ridiculously simple act of accepting the forgiveness of our sin because of the work of Christ on the cross, a stopping of our struggle to be good as the path to the goodwill of God. This gift of righteousness is what gives us the *right* to come to God in prayer, the *right* to expect that God will answer our prayer, and the whole basis of this right is that we have been united with Christ and, in a sense, it is Christ who is praying with and through us. If you would like a biblical expression of this, read Galatians, Ephesians and Hebrews. Would one expect a prayer from Christ to be unanswered? That is the first aspect of Salvation.

Furthermore, if, as St. Paul writes, "Christ is our wisdom, our righteousness our sanctification and our redemption", then it is clear that righteousness is not something that we can generate, create, or work towards in our own strength. The only thing that God expects from us is the realization that everything related to salvation is a gift of God. It is the divine assertion that nothing we do can effect/bring about, either our forgiveness or the transformation of our heart. It is not in a human's ability to transform him/herself into the holy nature of God or deal with the sinfulness within the heart of each one of us. Forgiveness, and all other aspects of salvation are the gift of God attained for us in and through Jesus.

The second aspect of salvation is the process of becoming holy, of changing our nature into the nature of Christ. This is called sanctification.

When Saint Paul in Galatians says, "I am crucified with Christ" do not ask, "How can this be? I am very much alive, and I am all too conscious of my sinfulness." *However, when* Jesus died he not only took our sins, as if these sins were a part, separate to ourselves. Somehow he also took all that we are and will be into himself in his suffering and death, and in this sense, as Paul tells us, we are all crucified with Christ.

It follows then that in his resurrection all that we are rose to new life with the risen Jesus. The resurrection of Christ is the resurrection of the entire human race (among other cosmic things). The entire human race is raised to new life in the resurrection of Christ. And yet it is simultaneously true that each one of us must turn from sin and accept this salvation gift achieved for us by Jesus on the cross, for as long as we continue to live "outside the gift of God" we are incapable of experiencing the new life of this gift of God. Perhaps, problematically, this Pauline teaching makes it impossible to imagine that it was not, indeed, the entire human race who died and rose again in Christ.

In the cross and resurrection we became united with Jesus in a spiritual union that obliterates the separation, the existential difference between Jesus and us, you and me. We see this union with Jesus clearly when Jesus says to Paul/Saul on the way to Damascus, "Saul, why do you persecute me?" Paul/Saul was persecuting the church.

However, How Do We Stop Being Sinful and Start Being Holy?

So if we are united with Christ and live in Him, if we allow this, if we stop trying to be holy, the life of Christ will surprisingly begin to be lived out in our lives. So how do we get out of God's way so that this life can be *revealed in and to us and to the world?* First we must completely surrender our will to God. That is, our heart must say to God, "your will not mine." Second, we must spend time with God so that he can heal and transform our hearts. Prayer is important, meeting with other believers is important, regularly reading the scriptures is important. Admission, confession of sin to God is important. If at all possible, there should be time when we silently put ourselves in God's presence so that he can work in our hearts.

But *none of these things*, as acts done, *earn* our transformation. The transformation of our nature comes about because the new life of Jesus, evidenced by the resurrection, Jesus (him) self, (the Holy Spirit of Jesus) transforms our hearts within us. As 2 Corinthians 3:18 tells us, " But we all with open face (with nothing obstructing our vision) beholding as in a mirror the glory of the Lord, are changed into the same image from glory (one state/level of holiness) to glory, even as by the Spirit of the Lord."

These things we do only open our hearts to God. They do not earn us points. The Pauline epistles, especially Romans, Galatians, Ephesians, Philippians, 1 Corinthians, and the anonymous book of Hebrews are crucial in helping us understand this way to a good nature, to holiness.

Jesus, thus, as a result of his work on the cross and through the resurrection, initiates a completely different "method" of character development that has no relationship, among other self directed activities, to determination, self-improvement and both positive or negative reinforcement as inputs to character change. I am not suggesting, on the other hand, that God does not force us to experience, sometimes harsh realities that hopefully cause us to change our behaviour.

Trying, A Certain Pathway to Failure

As long as one attempts to become holy by one's own efforts, either as a Christian or as a non-Christian, the nature of God never becomes one's nature. The church has had, and continues to have a very poor understanding of how the believer becomes holy. The tendency to try to make oneself holy, however, is a very natural tendency, especially when one realizes that God expects us to express a holy character. Additionally, we have been socialized to believe that what we are results from our own decisions and that we alone must change our behaviour.

Nevertheless, it is the Spirit of God working in us that produces God's nature, and this is why Christians are different to non-Christians. *This, and this alone, is the consistent and uniform method/process whereby human beings become good.* And this is why Christians have no reason to boast or feel superior to other human beings if they seem to be morally better than others.

Are Christian Values Radically Contrary to Societal Feelings, Beliefs and Behaviours?

However, the more one begins to think about the implications of Jesus' words in regards to how we interact with and view other human beings, the more one becomes increasingly overwhelmed by the seeming "impossibility" of following his directions in our relations with society. Indeed, I suspect that if society were to follow these divine directions, the world of human personal, social, political and legal interaction would come to an almost total abrupt crashing halt.

For the Christian, the question this raises is, "to what extent should the Christian cut him/herself off from socially normal

and accepted behaviours that are contrary to these divine implications?" Is it, in fact, even possible to do so? Does Christianity
actually have a Weltanschaung, a worldview that is seriously,
truly, radically different to that of our society, and is it possible
to reify, make, create this in a non-Christian society?

Is Even the Organization of the Church a Corrupting Influence?

Furthermore, does Christianity become inevitably cor-
rupted as soon as it becomes organized and bureaucratic?
Indeed, does Christianity become, perhaps even more corrupt
as soon as it attempts the "high and holy" goal of creating a separate, lasting and genuine Christian society, or is the believer
forced to attempt to follow Jesus' directions only on the individual level?

Is Holiness Simply the Way We Treat Others?

Our possession of a holy/good nature and how we view
others are intrinsically connected. Unfortunately, I suspect that
the world, and this must assuredly include the majority of the
world's religious people, is not willing to view others as God
does, and this is the cause of virtually all the social problems
we must confront.

There is no difference between Jesus' command to do unto
others as we would have them do to us, and his comment that
the fulfillment of the Law is to love God with all our hearts and
love our neighbour (with as much, or even more love than we
love) our self.

What is The Crucifixion of the Self?

This, incidentally, expresses Jesus' much misunderstood idea of the crucifixion of the self, (a self that, like some all encompassing black hole sucks all to itself) and becomes, rather, radically and entirely 'other' oriented, a "crucified" self that most of us have very little conception of, and posit, almost like dark matter, as necessarily possible, but virtually unknown.

What It is Not, and What it Is

The crucifixion of the self is not a titanic struggle to destroy evil in one by determination and the crushing of the self's evil desires. It is not a battle that one wages against oneself. Rather it is the transformation of one's being into one in which the nature of Jesus becomes one's inner, true nature. This is, essentially, the teaching of the crucifixion and resurrection of the human race in Jesus. In fact, the presupposition of the crucifixion of the self is the achievement of the Saviour on the cross and through the resurrection. If "I am crucified with Christ", as Paul states in Galatians, then, potentially, the crucifixion of the self is the crucifixion of Christ.

Does the scripture not teach us that we cannot achieve this in our own strength, through determination and a deeper and deeper commitment? Romans 5:6 makes this very clear when Paul writes "For at the very time when we were still powerless, then Christ died for the wicked." We are not simply forgiven and then left to our strength of will to transform ourselves. Paul asserts that we are powerless to acquire a holy character and that the only power we do have is the life of Christ within the believer.

If This is So, Does the New Testament Assert That Humans Do not Have the Power to Change Their Character?

Don't humans, or at least some of us, have the will power to change our behaviour? The answer must surely be 'yes'. However, if Paul is correct, the goodness we achieve in our own strength is not the holiness of God. Our true, self oriented nature has not been transformed into the nature of Christ, and changing 2 Corinthians 5:17 into the negative, "old things have not passed away and all things have not become new".

There are two people who can achieve change in the character of the individual: you and Jesus. The nature of the change so achieved will, however, be different. If it is true that we are "powerless" then what 'we' achieve will not be radical enough. St. Paul perhaps, is even more explicit, and writes, "Scripture has declared the whole world to be prisoners in subjection to sin" so that faith in Jesus Christ may be the ground on which the (prophetically) promised blessing is given. (Galatians 3:22 NEB) What this tells us is that both forgiveness and holiness are not achieved through determination and rigorous commitment to the development of a good character.

Good character is not, however, to be mocked. Indeed, those who seek to lead a meaningful, unselfish and other driven life are to be admired. Nevertheless, the path of inner struggle and determination is not the divine pathway.

This is inescapably clear from Paul's description of his life before encountering Christ.

> "If anyone thinks to base his claims on externals, I could make a stronger case for myself. ... in my attitude to the Law, a Pharisee; in pious zeal a persecutor of the church; in legal rectitude (character and obedience to the Mosaic law) faultless. But all such gains I have written off because of Christ. (Philippians 3:4-7)

The truly difficult reality this teaches is that sadly, both the goodness humanly attained and the method(s) used to attain this goodness are inadequate and ineffective. You either believe Paul or you don't.

If a blameless character was sufficient criterion for God, Paul/Saul had more than enough. Yet, he declares that all his humanly achieved goodness was a dead end, useless, the wrong path. Moreover, the truth is that the population of the world, from the beginning to the present, has never totally perfected themselves, even to the level of Saint Paul as Saul. And Saul/Paul in evaluating the nature of that perfection, judged even that level of goodness as still inadequate, still in its deepest nature, sinful. Quite simply, what Paul claims is that only with the indwelling Christ, can a person become a truly good person that it is through the indwelling Christ transforming the heart, reprogramming it, that one's nature becomes the nature of God.

However, surely it is obvious that one's nature does not immediately become holy in the instant of becoming a Christian. Rather, like a sick person who has several or many maladies, each is treated severally, until all are "healed". So this transformation does not occur all at once. Rather, "we are changed from glory to glory by the Spirit of the Lord". There is so much in the heart that needs to be healed and 'reprogrammed', and God deals with us, often gradually and in steps.

This is Not How the World Thinks of Behavioural Change

This, non-self centred way of living, however, is not how the world works, and it is sadly not how most Christians and the church itself work.

The Hermeneutical Problems of Biography and Poetic Expression

Indeed, to return to the original questions, how can we arrive at a true understanding of another human being (let alone ourselves) if we do not have all the information necessary for such an understanding? The person one imagines a poet to be is almost certainly unlike the real person who is the creator of the poems. Our difficulty is simply that our perception of the poet is incomplete, that the poetry, at best, reveals only a limited number of possible aspects of the poet/person.

In addition, as far as biography is concerned, even after more than a hundred or even hundreds of pages of biography, what kind of person is revealed? Is the complete person depicted in these tales of life? What has been omitted? Why, indeed, were certain details, thoughts, feelings and experiences left out? Also, in the attempt to make the text literary, in other words aesthetically attractive, is reality somehow altered? Furthermore, to what degree is the writer attempting to protect him/herself from the reader?

Finally, doesn't the omission of any experience, thought etc. make the 'picture' of the biographer inaccurate, and do these omissions not suggest that these omitted aspects are the very aspects that would allow a true and accurate understanding of the writer? On the other hand, do we have a right to a "true and accurate" understanding of the writer, and in what sense does "all the information" give us a true and accurate understanding? Indeed, if we did possess all the information, would be able with all this data to interpret it accurately? Would not our biases and unconscious assumptions skew the interpretation? Furthermore, is there a necessary and positive value in possessing such knowledge?

Yet, with every line, every paragraph, a more complete picture of the author is surely revealed. The weakness in the disclosure of these pieces of data, however, is that to make an understandable picture they need to be interpreted. In other words, "what do they mean?" And interpretation, as has been suggested, is invariably open to the subjective positions, attitudes and biases through which this data is filtered. We have only to look at the completely contradictory interpretations of a politician's words and actions to see that this is so.

I suspect we all wish we could reveal all, absolutely all that we are, so that we could be accepted and loved, without the fear that another's knowledge of who we are will result in our rejection. I suspect this because I do not know anyone who enjoys being misunderstood. Of course, the general opinion is that such a complete self-revelation is "dangerously" impossible, and generally speaking, I feel this is true.

The Work

> *Though perhaps it seems not so, there is unity*
> *Though there is unity, perhaps it is not so.*

If I could advise someone who has older relatives to ask one question it would be, "Tell me what you did when you were young." Almost certainly this will lead to other questions. The older generation of one's family knows and has stories of their generation, and at times generations before them, and with their death, these will be forever lost. And yet I suspect almost no one asks their parents and grandparents questions of this nature. It seems unfortunately true that most of us do not possess any curiosity about our forbears until it is too late. Looking up genealogies is simply familial archaeology, and results only in the bones of knowledge, where we are left with inference, the only tool we can employ to give some kind of life and humanity to these ancient names.

What I am attempting is to answer a question I have not been asked.

> *Looking down the path*
> *we always walked.*
> *Is there*
> *even one stone that says*
> *we once were here?*

I have been told my grandmother wanted me to be named Dudley Herbert. I suspect I would not have survived such an august appellation among my young classmates. Fortunately, my mother saved me from such a fate. As it turned out, when I was a child my life outside our family life was quite happy. I,

1

and all but one of my brothers and sisters, were born in Sydney. It was here that most of our ancestors came to, lived and died. And so it is that, more than any other place where I have ever lived, Sydney is home.

My first memory is of a hole under a side fence of our house at the edge of the bush, on Mowbray Road in Lane Cove that my sister and I hoped would let us trap a rabbit. I have no other memories of this house but I possess ration cards for this address for butter and sugar that allowed my mother to be sold these items. This must have been just a few years after the end of World War 2 when Australia had not yet freed itself from its wartime economy.

I do not know where my father got the money but some-time after this he bought a business in Neutral Bay. Perhaps he had saved his Air Force pay for the years he was in the RAAF and had bought the house in Lane Cove with this, and had then used this to buy the business in Neutral Bay. This sounds at least reasonable. This was directly opposite the now long gone tram depot and consisted of the shop on the main floor and some kind of arrangement above, where we all lived. I do not remember if my younger brother and sister had been born at this point but they may have been.

My sister and I went to a public school not far from our business but my only academic memory of this school, whose name I have completely forgotten, is being in a special class because I could not say "r". Instead of saying "rabbit" as I am now perfectly able to do, I would say "wabbit", cute per-haps, but obviously wong. I believe we both came home on our own, though this may be maligning my mother's activities in this regard.

On the other hand we did have a great deal of freedom to move about. When I failed to come home on time one afternoon my mother discovered me with my back to the wall, probably of a garage, and surrounded by a pack of barking dogs. This did not endear me to the species.

There was a fish and chip shop just a little way down the street from our business and I remember going there to buy some deep fried and battered slices of potato which I believe, in Australia, are called scallops, though I am willing to stand corrected on this.

Each Saturday afternoon my parents would walk us all down to the theatre to watch the two Saturday afternoon matinee movies. One of these would be Batman and Robin or Superman, or perhaps Tarzan and the other movie would often be a cowboy film. There would also be a newsreel and a cartoon. Sometimes in all this entertainment the audience would be encouraged to "follow the bouncing ball" and sing along with a song being played on the screen. At some theatres an organ would rise up out of the depths at the front of the theatre and play for the audience before the films were shown. This was all that remained of the time of silent movies when the theatre had to provide the musical background to the silent film. All of this came with the inexpensive price of the matinee ticket.

It's more than half a century now
I ran down the street
in Neutral Bay
my coat billowing out
a tiny Superman
Batman for a moment
pretending
after the Saturday afternoon
movie matinee
my parents took us to
each week.
They were young
and I had years to go
to reach their age,
almost as old
as my father

when he died of a
broken heart.
So many fights between
them and now,
so much pain and unhappiness.
He was so young
and she still full of dreams
and I
no longer young myself
and looking at my own life
think one more time
of theirs
and life's inevitable
answer to pain.

In about 1951 our family sold the store and moved 630 miles north to Brisbane. We children discovered that the adults had bought a newsagency business and a house, and though I remember the trip up to Brisbane in a car (when did my father get a car?) I cannot recollect moving into the house or how I felt about our exodus from our birthplace. Actually, we may have moved north in 1950 for the first year at our new school was not called grade one but rather, prep one, and though I skipped one level somewhere after grade one, I am not certain about when it all began. I simply know that I completed grade eight in 1958.

The street on which we lived in Cannon Hill, as our suburb was called, and the one due south that could be reached through an empty lot between two houses, were a little unofficial village. Though not all were acquaintances, we knew the people around us, what they occasionally did and many of their names. One of our neighbours apparently died of a stroke while sitting on his outside toilet. As you can imagine, one is constantly reminded of such an embarrassing place to die. How we got this information I have no idea because we did not visit anyone, except for the immediate neighbours to the right of our house and my friend's house on the next street south.

These neighbours to our right lived in a very small house that may have been, at one time, a railway carriage. They were friendly to us and I remember the wife giving me some first day covers for my stamp album. I immediately ripped off the stamps making the gift of no value. Naturally, I did not tell her what I had so foolishly done.

On the other side of our house was an empty bakery in which we, in innocent ignorance of the law, used to play. I say 'play' yet that is not the correct word. I cannot recall any games or imagined activities that we 'played'. We wandered around the empty building, picking up unused receipts and then finding the building uninteresting, left. Perhaps my friend imagined fun things to do in the building but strangely, I could not. I think we really went there because it was strange, unlocked and mysteriously empty. It had a great pile of unburnt coke next to our fence, though we didn't really know what to do with it. This sense of impotence always filled me with a feeling of waste. I think Dance, the owner, must have closed down this, now long gone bakery when they built a new, larger one…also in Cannon Hill.

Somehow, we also knew the neighbours to the back of our house though I, at least, had never had any social contact with them. I remember once, when my father was going away, possibly to visit family, though as he had a rather demanding business I don't know how he could have gone away, that my parents arranged with another neighbour about four houses up from us, to start our car periodically so that the battery would not run down, at least that was the reason as I remember it.

All of us children used to walk to school, about a mile or so away, and to do this we had to walk past a house that was directly in our way to school. It could not be avoided. In this house were two men who were believed to be insane. They may have been simply extremely mentally handicapped. I don't think either of them ever did anything, and my memory of them is only that they acted strangely, wore almost no clothes, and were therefore rather scary.

My friend, who lived in a house almost directly opposite the small store we owned on their street, was three years older than I. It was he who taught me to tie a Windsor knot for my tie. Surprisingly, though I clearly remember his mother, I do not believe, in all the years I knew my friend, I ever met his father. We both ended up at the same high school, not in our neighbourhood. Arrogantly, I cannot but believe, we looked down on him in regards to his intellectual abilities, though this was clearly unfounded, as he went on to acquire two or three degrees and was quite successful in the Uniting church ministry. Surprisingly, we still communicate and he is still my friend.

How we became acquainted I cannot recall. However, we played a lot together. There was an empty, very small house at the back of our store and we dug a square hole in the earth in front of this house, the object of which, we discovered, was beyond our childish abilities and we gave up the attempt. Why we didn't play in the empty house and rather felt we needed to dig a hole in the ground instead seems a mystery.

We lived at the edge of the city, and at the end of our street were paddocks and some bush with a small creek we used to jump over in our games. We had unformed and definitely unthought out plans to build a fort in this bush, so I would take our blunt little tomahawk axe and we would cut down paperbark trees that we were going to make the fort with. Of course, we never really planned what to do with these trees. We discovered there were snakes in these fields, which may have been poisonous, but happily we never thought about that possibility either.

All this semi-farm land was for fattening cattle that had been transported by train from outback cattle stations and had lost weight in being transported. There was a large abattoir on the Brisbane River a mile or so from where we lived and it was here that all these cattle met their unhappy end. My father used to deliver newspapers to this place, and once I went with him in my cub uniform, going onto a large oceangoing ship docked there, walking around and talking to some of the crew that would take the dressed meat, probably to England.

Quite near this huge meat processing factory was a series of multi-floored wooden buildings that earlier may have been used as barracks for soldiers during the war, but at this time were used to house migrants to Australia until they presumably found their own places to live.

Our suburb was, in fact, quite militarily oriented. Apart from the bases, several of the streets in our neighbourhood obviously alluded to the military: Gatling, Shrapnel, our street was named Moncrieff, probably after Gladys Moncrieff, Nordenfeldt (a kind of machine gun used in the Boer War) and Grenade St., and that is ignoring the very name of our suburb.

Though it did not occur to me then, the war had been over for less than ten years, and two military bases continued to operate in our otherwise peaceful suburb. One, immediately across from the local suburban railway station, was a fairly large Air Force base shaped in a kind of inverted L that had three or four old bombs placed around a flagpole at the entrance to the base. The other base, near the buildings used for the migrants, was an army camp, I think, and though we delivered newspapers to the air-force base, we had almost no involvement with it.

My friend and I used to ride our bikes down to the riverside just along from the army base and sit on an old Second World War landing craft that lay at right angles to the river. Though it, no doubt, would have been an ideal place to go fishing, it never entered our minds to try this. This lack of imagination seems to have been a common trait with both of us as we also appeared to have little interest in the details of this (there may, in fact, have been two of these) landing craft other than to sit on it and watch what was happening on the deep muddy river flowing by that had clearly seen much activity in the last war.

Growing up.
"She loves me George.
She doesn't love you."
The paradigm for human relating.
O Grandma!
If only I could have stayed
twelve years old
and visited you each summer.
How cool and fresh the water was
in your old fashioned bathroom
with the bath that stood
on four lion's paws.
Then I could have avoided
the hateful callousness
of adulthood
the endless string of fights with my wife
and the empty feeling of a life
not even Karl Marx
would have thought acceptable,
despite its totally materialistic bent.
How I wish I could walk again
through the cattle fattening paddocks,
jump over the slimy creek
and senselessly chop down paper bark trees,
get on my bike
ride to the edge of the river
with no one wondering where I was
and sit with my friend
on the side of the old landing craft,
rusting out its days on the bank of the Brisbane.
Then I only had to contend with
my drunken father.
Little did I realize what life was like
when you grow up.

To the right, and parallel to the landing craft was a large, deep, rectangular water filled "thing" that had been cut into the rock. We always imagined that it had been used for submarines, yet this was clearly impossible as the end close to the river was solid rock. Nevertheless, given the proximity of all things military around and nearby, it almost certainly had been made for the military. Indeed, there was an American army camp in Bulimba, the suburb in which the LC and the water filled 'tank' were situated, so both of these remnants may have been part of this camp. During the war large naval vessels and hospital ships had sailed up the river and docked, probably to resupply and be repaired. After all, Brisbane had been the headquarters for the South Pacific Allied Commander, Douglas MacArthur.

There may have been times when we walked here, or to another place nearby, for I remember having to cross a field that often had cattle in it. To me this was always a fearful experience. Two roads joined each other at the road that led to the abattoir and created this triangular field so that in order to save walking the two sides of the triangular field we would cross the bottom side of the triangle, avoid stirring up the cattle, and save quite a walk. Performing this fearful act was not an expression of courage, but rather the result of laziness in the face of inconvenience. Once across this frightening shortcut we could walk down towards the LC where there was an ordinary looking house which sold tropical fish in large tanks outside the house and all sorts of wild birds.

A few streets away from our house, close to where a large elevated railway bridge crossed the main Wynnum road, there was another of the tiny creeks that criss-crossed our suburb. This little marshy creek was the home of small fish about two inches long, and at various times the home of scores of black tadpoles. The adult purpose of the fish, they were not natural to the waters, was to eat mosquito larvae. We children used to try to catch the fish with little nets that were usually made out of any available material we had as we walked past and noticed the fish.

The tadpoles almost certainly grew into hundreds of ugly poisonous toads that used to appear after dark and provide us with so much fun by throwing them onto the road where they would be run over, complete with sound effects, by oncoming cars. They were a pest, but that was not why I did this. They were ugly, and I never thought of the cruelty this obviously expressed. There were at least two kinds of pretty little green tree frogs that no one treated this way. The unequal treatment was never questioned.

This bucolic existence was quite enjoyable. Life in our house was less so. My parents used to argue/fight all the time (I speak as a child) and my father who was clearly unhappy, if not an alcoholic, used to get drunk, usually on the weekend at the local RSL, the veterans' club, or some hotel. He would then come home and later go to his business, roll hundreds of newspapers, load them into the car and then drive around the neighbourhood delivering them. How he successfully accomplished this in his condition is beyond me.

One Saturday he came home drunk and began angrily to smash a couple of windows. My mother took hold of us all and together we ran off down the street ending up at a flat roofed house whose occupant she obviously knew, though I didn't, and asked the lady if we could stay there for a while as my father was drunk and smashing things. Why she chose this lady's house for refuge I do not know and I never again had any other social interaction with this woman. I suppose the rest of our little community eventually got to know of this incident, just as we eventually got to know of their escapades, and that my mother had gotten to know her from the little store she managed on the same street.

I was frequently employed in my father's newspaper business and used to get up at 4 o'clock, drive to a house near our business listening to horrible hillbilly music, the only music on at that time, and pick up someone, can't remember why, and help him put the newspapers through a machine that rolled them up. We would then drive out and I would throw various newspapers onto the lawns of the people who had ordered them. Sunday newspapers were different to weekly papers and after a week of delivering one set of orders I would invariably forget who got the Sunday papers. I do not think this pleased my father.

About one hundred yards away from our business was a street called, I believe, Barrack Road, which intersected the main highway. Often, when my wife is cutting my hair, I find myself in the barber shop a little way down this road, a young boy sitting in the large swivelling barber's chair loosely covered from the neck down by what, at one time, may have been a sheet, getting my hair cut. I feel it must have been a rather pleasant, relaxing experience because otherwise it has almost no significance.

A short walk down this road were the Air Force base and the suburban train station on a perfectly straight road that eventually led down to Lytton Road, an alternative way to Moreton Bay, and where, almost immediately there arises a steep hill I had to force myself to climb whenever I rode my bicycle the fourteen odd miles to Wynnum, and which my father took to get to a little wilderness popularly called Lytton Wall that ran along the bank of the Brisbane river a short distance along this road. Just before the wall we could collect purple cactus pears, then go fishing, and where he once hooked me as he attempted to cast out into the river.

During the week, after delivering the morning papers, I would then go home, eat breakfast, and walk to school. To get to school, after successfully passing the "crazy house", we had to walk under a low railway bridge that crossed a small creek about half a mile from the railway station and the challenge, when a train was passing, was to avoid getting showered on by boiling steam expelled from the train as it crossed the short bridge. This dangerous possibility may well have been the product of our childish imaginations.

Once on the other side of the railway bridge we walked though a very large, open grassy field that acted, I suspect, in much the same manner as the common would in pre-industrial England. It was on this that the community celebrated Guy Fawkes Day each year, building a large bonfire, similar to the ones people were burnt alive in, in the dark days of history. I don't remember if we made a scarecrow like model of Guy Fawkes, indeed, almost certainly we did not, given the barbaric associations that would have engendered, but the great fire would be lit and large amounts of fireworks would be set off to everyone's glee. It was also here that the circus would stay and perform when it came to town.

After we left the great field it was just a short walk to the school. Each morning before classes began, the entire school would assemble, class by class, on the open "parade" ground at the front of the school. The Head Master (principal) would give us information about what we were going to do as a school, we would sing God Save the Queen, and then we would be sent off to our classes to the accompaniment of well known marching music. It sounds, perhaps, more military than it actually was.

In the Head Master lay the power of ultimate punishment. Ordinary teachers, I suspect, did not have the right to physically punish a student. If such a punishment was needed the student would be sent to the Head Master's office to be caned. The bamboo cane was about three feet long and a quarter of an inch thick and the student would receive a maximum of six strikes against his upturned palms. The odd thing was, however, I don't remember in all the years I was at this school, more than two students ever being caned, and never the six possible strokes. I do not think any of the teachers, including the Head Master, wanted or believed in this method of disciplining.

Before grade one there were four "prep" levels. I do not know what the prep levels were intended to do other than to, obviously, prepare everyone for "going to school". Perhaps it was a combination of kindergarten and Montessori. My teacher in whatever prep level I was in was a Mrs. Black, and I have no negative memories of her. In the level I was put in, (I have no recollection of what that was) and also in grade one, we did not write on paper with a pencil or pen, but rather, on a slate. This was a thin rectangular piece of slate with a wooden frame about six inches by eight inches, and on this we wrote using a thin pointed piece of grey material, which may also have been slate. It left a white line on the slate, which was removed quite simply with a small piece of wet sponge. I cannot recall what grade finally began to use paper, but it was either grade two or three. I probably wrote more legibly using the slate than I did using paper, for I am sure I must be one of the world's most illegible writers.

Compared to the "green" school it now is, there was a great deal of open, even grassless space on which we were supposed to learn Maypole dancing. I could never understand the point of this dance, and quickly forgot what they had tried to teach us. Learning maypole dancing in Australia would be equivalent, I suspect, to teaching students in Britain to sing Waltzing Matilda. Some children used to come to school with bare feet. I suspect their families were not too well off, but this was never commented on. Once, I, and possibly others of my brothers and sisters picked up head lice, almost certainly from some of the other students, and each day my mother had to wash our hair with some medicine and then carefully comb it with a fine tooth comb. Fortunately, this was not a repeated problem.

At one part of the fence bordering the school and a neighbour's land was a small chicken run. I'm not sure how many of us played with this idea but every so often I and a couple of my friends would ineffectually attempt, to grab these chickens through small holes in the fence. It was not that we planned to steal a chicken. Rather, it was, "These chickens are so close. Can we grab one as it comes close to the fence?" To a 10 or 12 year old, the world was filled with a multiplicity of things to be experienced. Apparently, private property was not a concept that played a part in our juvenile thinking.

At the back of the school grounds was a large playing field. To the left end was a cement cricket pitch where the cricketers practiced, at the far side was a small decline where, during breaks, students would dig for sweet potatoes, though I never saw any, and the rest was a large area for football or field hockey. It was not called field hockey because no one knew anything about ice hockey. When students were playing hockey anybody could join in, and there was no fixed number on either team. We played with hockey sticks and if we didn't have the good fortune to own one of these, just long pieces of stick. It was pure fun. The day I finally got a real hockey stick was a great day, even if I was a less than stellar player.

We had two businesses, the small one mentioned previously, run by my mother, and a larger one on the main road to Wynnum. About a hundred yards from our store, was a rectangular water trough, roughly 18 inches by 60 inches and 18 inches deep, for horses. I have no idea how old this was, but though I never saw anyone riding a horse anywhere in our suburb, the trough was always full of water. Our business was a newsagency cum vegetable store and stood in front of a house that belonged to one of my best friends. His parents owned the hardware store next to ours. They were Jehovah's Witnesses, though this impacted our friendship not at all. He was the smartest kid in the class, and though sometimes he and I traded places according to marks for first and second, he was definitely first more often than I was. Years later I met him in the Christian bookstore I used to go to quite often. I acknowledged him but made no attempt to initiate a conversation. It was as if the time of our earlier friendship meant nothing. I wish I could ask my friend for his forgiveness for this. It was not that I felt something negative about my friend. My mind was totally empty of any response to seeing him.

I was a completely "good" kid at school, and the only time I was punished was in grade six for illegible writing. He and I used to play cricket in his yard, though once his mother angrily came out and stopped us for some unknown adult reason. My family and local kids also used to play cricket on the street in front of our house, often until it was too dark to see the ball. I loved this game, but played for my primary school only once, accidentally making one run.

My other friend was a half Russian half Chinese boy who was so tall at the age of twelve that bus drivers would not believe he was not an adult. Every couple of weeks or so he and I would go by bus to the Vulture Street public library, the nearest library at that time, the bus shaking and groaning as its powerful old engine pulled away from each stop. Quite often I would go to his house on Wynnum road, and his grand-mother would take us both down to her room and try to teach us Russian. His mother had been Miss Shanghai and she would feed us Chinese food and teach me how to use chopsticks. They were Jewish, and each Passover we would eat matzo, unleavened bread.

I know not why but he had lent one pair of ivory chopsticks and a silver pair to one of the students in our class. This student owed me money for some long forgotten debt, and to pay me he "gave" me my friend's two pairs of chopsticks. I do not remember if I understood this little bit of dishonesty on his part. Anyway, I kept the chopsticks for perhaps thirty or forty years and later, when my friend and I were both much older I offered them back to him. The mistake was years in the past and he told me to keep them, after all they had very little value and he had forgotten all about the incident. I have used many different pairs of chopsticks, but I have never used these. Once, when I was going away on a trip, I hid them, and now I have no idea where they are, except that they must be somewhere in my study.

There were fields and bush all around his house at that time, and a little creek that had freshwater crayfish. About two lots further along the road my friend lived on was a dirt road called Creek Road that intersected the main road. It is now a multi-laned paved road that runs beside a huge shopping mall, and I would be very surprised if the creek is not now covered by a housing development, and no one knows that a creek where crayfish lived, once flowed where they now live. One time, when we were down near the creek, he "dared" me to eat a really hot chilli. I licked it, perhaps once, and my mouth filled with fire. I stood up and ran like an idiot about a mile down the highway to our store, my mouth still on fire from the chilli. Not amusing.

Strangely, (with this, and my other friend) we never discussed what high school we were going to attend and I never thought of saying good-bye to him at the end of primary school. As it turned out, he and I went to different high schools after grade eight and I lost contact with him completely. The next time I heard of him he was in the UK leading a protest against something or other. He had become a communist, which must be a little funny, as his family had fled Russia to China to escape the communists. He later became an ABC cameraman and documentary producer.

I never fought anyone in elementary school except one boy who hated my father for completely imaginary reasons and apparently therefore hated me. One afternoon, on the way home from school, this kid picked a fight with me. I had no idea how to fight and so he was slightly beating me up when Walter, the younger brother of my Russian Chinese friend came and rescued me. The inglorious nature of my rescue was completely lost on me.

While I was in primary school I remember being in love with two girls. There may have been more but if there were I've forgotten them. The first girl was named Doris Muller and we were in grade four, possibly grade three. She was blonde, and as far as I was aware had no idea I liked her. Being the kind of person I was, I schemed to become friends with her brother. This worked, and one day I ended up at their house after school. We were in his room playing some childish game when she came in and he knowingly said, "go away. He's not interested in you." She replied, "Yes, he is". Did I follow up on this? Of course not. Nor did I ever go back to her house.

The next girl I liked was Brenda Stone, and apart from her prettiness, she had come from NSW and this put her ahead of any Queenslander. I think I was in grade seven at this point, which may lead the reader to suppose I now knew something about love and girls. This conclusion would be completely wrong. Swearing he would not tell anyone my secret that I liked BS, my best friend, the moment school ended for the day shouted across the street to her that I liked her. She replied that she also liked me. Did it occur to me to cross the street and walk home with her? The thought never entered my head.

The next Saturday afternoon at the Morningside movie theatre I discovered she was there with her friends. I bought an ice-cream with the idea that I would give it to her, but I was so afraid that I sat down on my own, and filled with fear let the ice-cream melt onto the floor. What a waste of two returned "loves".

Movies were an important part of our family's life. My father would take all the family to the movies two or three times a week. There was no television, and we would all go to the Morningside theatre, or the theatres at Hawthorne or Balmoral, all nearby suburbs, depending, of course, on the movie that was playing. I am certain these theatres no longer exist. One time we were at the Hawthorne theatre which was showing a movie titled, "It's Easy to Love". Part way through the movie I could not take this any more and my father and I both left the theatre. This was most unusual, for my father and I would never normally do something so feelingly together. I think, though probably we did not understand it at the time, that neither of us could endure any more, the painful longing to be loved that the film aroused, and had to walk out. At the time, the feeling I had was that the film was too "sucrose". When we got outside there were two huge great Danes walking along the footpath. We both waited outside in the dark until the film ended, and the rest of the family joined us and we went home.

Christmas in our house was usually a happy time. A pillow case would be put at the end of our beds and in the morning we would discover Christmas presents in it. I do not believe we imagined Santa Claus had been responsible for this generosity, though I suspect it began that way. The only present I remember was a crystal set. My brother and I were both given one, and if I remember correctly, there was some kind of simple aerial attached to the back of a plastic box about three inches deep and five inches long. How this worked I have no idea, but by turning a circular dial in the front we could pick up radio stations. It was a lot of fun as I lay in bed in the darkness listening to the radio, and surely one of the simplest devices imaginable.

At Christmas dinner we had, among other things, a dome shaped steam pudding into which, my father, had put sixpences and thrupences (small six and three penny silver coins). Onto this was poured plum pudding sauce, but the most important thing for each child was to find some money in the piece of pudding we had been given. My youngest brother continues this tradition, I believe, but later collects the coins, as they are no longer available as currency.

Having written all the negative things I have said about my father, two memories keep resurfacing of a completely opposite nature, memories that have let me see him in a surprisingly softer light. Sometime, almost certainly before I became a teenager, my father taught my brothers and sisters and me to play canasta. This is a card game involving two decks of cards, and at the time I thought it was a rather difficult game to understand, but we all played, usually on Saturday nights. I think even my mother played some Saturday nights. I cannot remember the rules of the game but it was clearly a lot of fun as we were never forced to play, and we did this for many Saturday evenings.

He also used to read to us all. He would sit in a large chair in the dining room and all of us children would sit around him at his feet. This must have made most of us quite happy as I remember one of us asked our father if we could call him "pop". He said that was fine but we should not call him "poppy". I can only assume that this shows we had some degree of affection for our father, and surely that he had, at the best of times, a fatherly affection for us.

This only makes the final calculation we all ultimately made of our father all the more sad. As I grew older I began to hate my father. Perhaps this feeling had been slowly growing within me from when I was a young child. My other brothers and younger sister apparently felt similarly. Probably this was inevitable from the drunkenness, the continual arguments with our mother and even acts and cruel evaluations of our childish behaviour that continued over the years until we all left home. I believe he could not control his feelings, and was depressed, perhaps most of the time. He tried, and probably reflecting the truth of the man, when I was told he had died, my first words were, "Well now he is no longer suffering".

During one winter, my grandfather stayed with us in the "warm north". When it came time for him to return to Katoomba, a smallish holiday town in the Blue Mountains sixty miles west of Sydney, it was arranged for my father to drive him home. It was also decided that I should accompany my father and I was consequently taken out of school, for however long this would take. We drove along the New England Tableland route, and it was here that I first saw snow. We had left quite early in the morning before the roads out of town became busy and I remember the darkness and the empty streets of the capital as we headed south. I doubt that I was ever told why I was to be part of this trip, but I wonder if it was my mother's unspoken attempt to keep my father from doing anything untoward. And, if so, was my father aware of this?

Rock'n Roll came to our school in 1955. I was in grade five and everyone, meaning all the kids in my class, was suddenly interested in music. We all listened to the top forty songs of the week on the radio, listening for the latest hit that most parents found repulsive.

Our grade five teacher, Mr. Graham, was a good man. He would play the Marseillaise as we "marched" into the music room. The fact that it was the French national anthem had nothing to do with anything. Once he asked us what our favourite song was and we unanimously cried out "Diana" by Paul Anka. He never made fun of the music we liked. Maybe he wasn't as old as we always imagined he was.

Rock'n Roll burst on the scene with "Rock Around the Clock". My friend down the street and I went to the Norman Park theatre to see the movie of the same name. This kind of music was like no other that we had grown up with. Sometime in the movie someone smashed a bottle against the wall. It was that kind of music.

Our house was a typical Queenslander, a one floor building off the ground on five-foot high round wooden posts about eight to ten inches across. This was to allow air to circulate through the house, especially during the hot summer months. It had a front enclosed veranda, a fairly large lounge, a dining room beside a good sized kitchen, a bedroom in the front for my parents and two bedrooms for my brother and me and my sisters. Some time in this family odyssey, for reasons they never found out, my sisters were sent away to a private girl's school near the Bay. My younger sister believes this was because my parents were thinking of buying a business about a hundred miles north in a little town I think was Gayndah. But why would they do this? Surely there were schools, even in that little town. Part of the front of the house was made into a bedroom for me. This may have been after my brother, ten years younger than I, was born.

We had a large frangipani tree in the front yard, a couple of fully grown poisonous but pretty oleander trees along the side fence, a mushroom shaped mango tree about twenty or thirty feet high in the back yard that we played in, but whose fruit I never ate because it was so messy, and a monstera deliciosa near the back where we had a chicken yard all along the back yard fence and about twelve feet wide. In the chicken yard were a lemon tree, a large fig tree that produced delicious black figs, and about fifteen or twenty chickens which regularly gave us eggs and occasionally, baby chickens. We also had a couple of roosters, one of which, named George, after my father finally caught him, ended up as a Sunday meal.

We did not have indoor plumbing back then. Each week or so a Hunter Brothers truck would come along our street, collect the cans full of human waste and replace the full cans with empty ones. What a revolting but necessary job. We had to go to this outside "dunny" away from the house, a most horrible and frightening place to go, especially at night. There was no light but occasionally there were spiders. Now I understand some of the reason we boys had "pissing contests" in the back yard. It was just easier.

My father built a flat open garage along the right hand side of the house and the roof of this was soon covered in wisteria. In grade four, apart from being in love with Doris Muller, the teacher handed out little silky oak trees and I planted mine in the middle of the back yard in front of the chicken run. It eventually grew into a large beautiful tree, though my parents may well have hated the tree as each year it dropped an enormous number of leaves that they had to clear up.

To get into our house from the back, one had to climb some wooden stairs. Little green grapes grew along one side of these stairs but they were always bitter and I never ate them, nor, I think, did anyone else. Attached to the back of the house was a large circular galvanized tank on a square wooden stand that collected wonderfully tasting rain water from the corrugated iron roof. When it rains in Australia it is usually rather loud and tumultuous but I always thought the sound of the rain beating on the corrugated iron roof was strangely beautiful and calming. The laundry was also in this vicinity, though I can't remember how this was located. Presumably the water tank was located after the laundry, which must have been connected to the back of the house.

The problem of how these two things were located is compounded by the fact that my father built a bird enclosure with a cement floor, about twelve feet by ten feet and maybe ten feet high in this area. In this enclosure he then built a cage about five feet wide and six feet high for budgies. The main enclosure was for parrots and apart from galahs and some Australian dove-like birds, I don't remember what kind of parrots we had, maybe red and green king parrots. My favourite parrot was and remains a crimson rosella, a bright red and blue parrot that my father called a mountain Lowry, but we never had any of these.

The door into this large cage was an ordinary house door and to feed the birds and give them water you had to open it. I was always afraid the birds would fly out but none of them ever did. Later I built a smaller birdcage behind the dunny, with logs on the ground. The cage held the birds but there were rats, which may have gotten some of the birds.

I never found out why, but my mother did not want me to have a cat. Obviously, against her wishes, I got a pretty white and yellow kitten anyway and this was accepted. Nor do I recall my mother being angry with me for this. We also had finches, guinea pigs, and dogs at various times, just mongrels, but the dogs, as well as the cat I imagine, never came into the house. One of our dogs was apparently killing some of the local people's chickens. My father, for reasons I will not evaluate, felt he had to kill the dog but he could not do this before he had drunk "enough" alcohol. Killing the dog must have deeply troubled him. After I came back from a cub camp, somewhere near Capalaba I believe, I found that my father had accidentally run over my cat with his car. It wasn't dead when I arrived home and it looked terrible. It died soon after. I am sure this saddened me.

Despite everything, it was my father, I believe, who taught us a love of the beauty of nature. He may have done this unintentionally, but I can discover no other strong cause for this feeling all my brothers and sisters possess.

Almost every Sunday afternoon in the summer he would take us swimming, either to Rainbow Bay or to Tallebudgerra Creek (really a river) near where it emptied into the ocean, both about sixty miles south on the Gold Coast. He would drive down the Pacific highway through Beenleigh, about half way to the coast, famous for its rum factory and its slightly ridiculous ads, sometimes buy a roasted chicken at a roadside store or pies at the Yatala pie shop and head south.

We spent two Easters at Rainbow Bay in a small wood frame house right across from the ocean, and two or three times, probably on the way to or from Sydney, we had holidays in a quite primitive collection of little cabins at Brunswick Heads, at a place we called "Harry's", though actually it was called Sheltering Palms, not too far across the Queensland-New South Wales border, with the ocean on one side and the Brunswick River on the other. Years later, a huge storm swept all these buildings into the river, never to be rebuilt.

In this freezing land
I watch the black cloud
slowly covering the numbers on the dial
that told the time
at Rainbow Bay.

Standing by the sea
on the shores of P.E.I.
I see the rolling green hills
the turn off to Mullumbimby
and up and around the bend
the ocean
and Brunswick Heads.

Harry's
To a place of ghosts and empty spaces,
to what no longer was,
I took my wife and child
and saw a twelve year old boy,
skinny and shy,
a row boat, pulled up at low tide,
my father and mother, now dead,
cooking breakfast in the grassy square
where once log cabins stood.
The leaves rustle in the breeze
and on the beach
the sound of waves.

We would row this little boat directly across the relatively narrow Brunswick River to the town that lay on the opposite bank. I do not think there was any particular reason for these trips other than for something to do. Of course there were grocery stores and restaurants and a distinguished but diminutive brick hotel, but the expedition was not really to resupply our refrigerator, as far as I can recall.

On the other hand, the boat allowed us to try fishing spots the locals had told us of. My father would occasionally row one or two of us, two or three hundred yards upriver with him to catch black bream. These fish used to eat a particular kind of moss that grew on rocks in the river and I always wondered how we could catch anything using this rather odd bait. Indeed, I don't remember that we ever did

Just off to one side at "Harry's" there was a kind of community hall, and several nights a week the owner would show movies for the people in his cabins. As the movies played, in the background one could hear strangely calming waves breaking on the beach, sounding like the muffled guns of distant artillery, harmful to no one, and between each breaker there would be a short regular silence, before the next wave broke.

At other times he would drive us into the countryside, turning off from the highway and driving along narrow winding country roads until he found a deserted grassy spot beside a pleasant looking creek where we would swim and play and have a wonderful relaxing picnic.

In those days, instead of a bridge across the numerous shallow creeks that one encountered, the government would lay a cement surface below the water level to splash over as one drove across. And before bridges replaced them, over some of the many rivers, five or six cars would drive onto small ferries to be pulled across by cables. Bridges have probably replaced all these ferries, but the romance and the quiet pace of this life have gone.

We certainly travel more efficiently, we drive more quickly, and we arrive much earlier, but I doubt we see much that we speed past, and I am not sure we come away with that quiet and unconscious accumulation of pleasant memories that, with age, promise to enrich our days.

I'm also fairly sure this will be poo pooed by the poor slaves of a constant stream of inescapable data and unimportant information, who all too often seem to view human contact only as ego driven repartee with witty put downs.... and cannot slow their hearts (and fingers) to silently watch, perhaps, the gentle lapping of waves against a barnacle encrusted pier, or take the time to watch breeze blown ripples flow across a field of grain...

but then, I don't know... But what kind of memories are they accumulating?

Once we stopped by a creek surrounded by hilly land and I decided to find what would happen if I rolled some smallish boulders down the hill. Fortunately no damage to car or people ensued, and watching the rocks crashing down the hill I thought this was delightful fun. Another, I suppose rather revolting game we played was throwing dry cow patties like Frisbees at any brother or sister who happened to be near. I suspect this shows that we were not completely "city" kids, for I cannot imagine city children even contemplating such a "game".

Occasionally my father would take my brother and me out shooting for the weekend. We slept on old army camp cots beside the car, and drank tea from a billycan boiled over our small fire where my father must have cooked our meals, though I cannot remember ever eating. At dawn we would walk quietly through the bush looking mainly for rabbits but we also saw wallabies, eagles, too many rabbits to mention and once a platypus. As we wandered around the country where we had stopped we sometimes found part of the skeleton of a cow or some other animal that had died. I don't know why but we did not think this was strange or horrible in any way...just part of the land. My father had a 12-gauge shotgun and we had 22's. He had hunted since he was a teenager and the rabbits he shot were to be eaten. He was a good shot.

However, until the time I started to feel that shooting was not a good practice, I usually missed everything. The truth is that we would shoot at anything that moved, and though this was usually rabbits, I remember shooting a wallaby which we skinned, discovering in the process that it was infested with worms. I tried rather ineffectually as it turned out, to scrape the fat from the inside of the skin, but I had this skin on the floor beside my bed for many years afterwards. At the point where I began to question what we were doing I began to hit what I fired at. Nevertheless, walking quietly through the dewy grass, as the sun was just rising, even if we found nothing, was an experience I look back on with no regret.

Standing inside
I look out at the frozen earth
where, finally
the snow
is almost gone.
A few sparrows sing
and the feel of Spring is
in the air.
But I know that
in Summer
I will not be driving down
to the beach
feel the hot white sand between my toes,
look out at the blue Pacific,
and watch the waves crash
in slowly rolling curves
out just beyond the calm,
or feel the heat rise
from the bush,
tinder dry
so hot you long for a cool creek
gurgling over mossy sandstone rocks
where you can lie
at last,
quietly,
in a shallow pool
overhung with eucalyptus and wattle
while the cries of wag-tails, whip birds,
scarlet king parrots and blue and red lowries
break the silence of the heat.
I know that
all too soon,

the leaves will fall,
and life again
take on the look of death,
freezing wind blow
over layers of snow
to bite into skin,
and every crunch of my boot
tell that
warmth has gone
while I,
apparently lacking the wisdom
of even ducks and geese,
feel compelled to remain
in this foreign land
I now call home,
one more year

After grade eight, the end of primary school, I went to
Brisbane State High School. This was the only state run school
included in the Greater Public Schools. There were ten, if I
recall, and it had a good academic record. All of us brothers
attended this school but the only one to graduate was my
youngest brother. Perhaps he had more perseverance. After
he graduated from high school he went on to Duntroon, the
Australian military college, and became the youngest lieutenant
in Australian military history. Fortunately, all of us later went
on to university, my younger brother becoming, for some time,
the private secretary to the Lord Mayor of Brisbane.

The first day of high school as we stood at parade, the
sub-juniors (grade 9s) at the left and the seniors (grade 12s) at
the right, as I looked across at the seniors, some in their formal
school jackets embroidered in gold with their athletics and academic achievements, I thought they were giants, and compared
to us, they were. My friend, with whom I had dug holes, cut
down paper bark trees and sat on world war two landing craft

beside a river, was in senior the year I was in sub-junior, but at school we almost never interacted socially. Come to think of it, even in elementary school we had never interacted at school. This was not a verbal arrangement we had discussed together. It simply did not happen.

To get to and from this school I had to catch an old steam train. I say it was old not because all this happened so long ago. Rather, it was old even when I was travelling in it. There was a thankfully short tunnel we had to pass through, and one had to close one's eyes and mouth to keep from getting particles of ash in one's eyes or mouth from the train engine. We had to wear school uniforms, and many was the time I had to scrunch my hat in one hand and clumsily run the half mile down the street, my heavy briefcase, full of books, going in all directions, in order not to miss the early train home.

I remember my first Latin class in SJ 4. The teacher, the class had named Brutus, taught us the present tense conjugation of the Latin verb "amo". My mother, who never spoke to me of her university experiences, wanted me, I believe, to take Latin because she had enjoyed this subject at Sydney University. Though I suspect she really should not have done this, my mother used to "help" me translate my Latin set pieces. She had majored in Latin and Roman law and I feel now that this must have given her some pleasure to use what she had worked so hard at, and perhaps loved. I wish I had been able to give her pleasure in enjoying it as she once had. I was never very good at Latin but almost certainly that is because I was lazy, or simply wasn't interested in making an effort in almost anything.

In my class in sub-senior I sat next to a student who shared an affection with our English teacher for Gilbert and Sullivan plays. Both of them knew vast passages of these plays by heart. For me, a truly incredible feat. During my time in this grade I was also in a tiny history class that had five students at the most. Our lesson was immediately after lunch, and for some reason I fell asleep during a lesson. One cannot hide in such a small class and I was woken up, but I cannot remember the choice words the teacher handed me.

At that time I was completely uninterested in history, and it was not until studying pre-modern Japanese history under Dr. Isao Soronaka at university that such a desire to learn was kindled. There are characters all around the world who are fascinating and worthy of the time it takes to discover their impacts on the world in which they lived, and indeed on our own world.

After reading about the military exploits of leaders and generals over the last four or five hundred years, in Europe, Asia and the United States, one begins to see patterns of behaviour in victory and defeat, in a leader's willingness and ability to take risks and plan strategically, in discrete battles, in the absolute importance of and destruction of military lines of supply in the effectiveness of military operations, and in the behaviour of the troops as a result of leadership, supplies, attrition and even their willingness to risk their lives.

If one learns the personal histories of leaders, and the political and economic policies they employ to develop, to build up reserves of all kinds in order to maximize the chance of future military success, studies unexpected political and military alliances in order to neutralize potential and future enemies, and observes the infrastructure, large and small, including logistical pathways they attempt to construct, one can begin to see possible future strategic economic and military ambitions.

These leaders do not need to be good people. In fact, they may be decidedly evil, but they can often teach us valuable lessons that are crucial to our self-preservation.

Clearly on a more mundane level, physical education periods were endurable, even if they were not particularly interesting. As part of this, once, and as far as I can remember only once, we were told we had to go on a long distance run around the school neighbourhood. Apart from the fact that we had never practiced for this, I had no desire at all to do this. So on the day we were supposed to run this course we all went into the change room, put on our phys ed clothing and began the run. I ran around the school (part of the designated track) ran back into the change room, put my school uniform back on, and went home. I have no idea if they ever found out that I had done this.

In my class there were two very clever students who, for their age, seemed to know everything about chemistry and physics. Confronted by their expertise I was embarrassed at my lack of academic uniqueness and decided to specialize in animal husbandry and become a dairy farmer, this despite the fact I had no real connection to the land. Predictably, this ambition soon withered, based as it was in such shallow soil. I also studied German, which did actually interest me.

I always tried to organize my time to cover all the subjects and usually passed everything but I never worked really hard and was never strongly motivated by anything.

In sub-junior, grade 9 in North American terms, Leighton Ford, a Canadian evangelist with Billy Graham, came to Brisbane. The school was encouraged, for some reason never explained, to go to a theatre near the school, possibly during lunch to hear him, and my friend, now in Senior (grade 12) the one who had tried with me to dig a hole to China or somewhere, and I were really impressed by what he said. We decided to go and hear him preach at the Milton tennis courts in town where he was holding the crusade. We both went out at the appeal at the end of the preaching. This simple act altered us for the rest of both of our lives. He was eventually ordained into the Methodist church.

Sub-junior and Junior I did not mind but I came to hate Sub-senior. I cannot remember why but I disliked my math teacher in sub-senior intensely. Whether he picked on me, or for some other reason, I cannot remember. Maybe he was just a miserable unfriendly teacher. On Friday afternoons the school had clubs for the students who were not military cadets. He was a major in the school army cadets. In sub-junior I had been in the

Air Force cadets of the Air Training Corps, a carry over from World War 2.

When I applied I only just got in. I was so short they had difficulty finding a uniform that was my size. I loved the Air Cadets, polishing my boots to a mirror shine, learning how to shoot a World War Two 303 rifle at the Air Force rifle range and going to cadet camp. My younger brother tells me that one night each week I would travel to an Air Force base, relatively far across the city, to construct a balsa wood model aeroplane. This I had indeed done, though I had not thought of this until he reminded me, many years later.

Though my father had been in the Air Force in World War 2, I don't recall ever talking to him about anything I did in the ATC, and yet I am sure that unconsciously I had joined the Air Cadets because he had been in the Air Force. At the end of the school year, after the passing out parade near the Exhibition grounds I walked all the way home across the city, in uniform, carrying my rifle.

Towards the end of sub-senior I was so unhappy I told my parents I wanted to leave school. Why they let me I do not know. Even though my father, as far as I know, had never finished high school because of the Depression, my mother had gone to the University of Sydney. Yet we were never encouraged to pursue any kind of academic path, or even to study hard.

For a while I muddled around not knowing what to do and then I got a job as a very junior clerk in the Co-ordinator General's department of the State government. This department, headed by the Premier of the state, organized and allocated funds for all the projects in the state of Queensland. In the mid 1940s, the department head before the one I worked for, had built the impressive Storey Bridge over the Brisbane River. In the course of time, I discovered that one of the senior clerks in my department had been a Desert Rat in North Africa, and later a POW after 25,000, British and Australian soldiers finally surrendered to the Germans, but to me he was too august to even imagine discussing such things with him. I worked there for about a year.

It was during that year I told my father I would not work anymore for him on Sundays because it was the Sabbath. His, probably quite natural response, was to tell me to leave his house. I couldn't have been happier. I have no idea what I would have done if my mother had not convinced him to change his mind, but in my thoughtless way of thinking, this did not please me.

My father certainly did things that helped me and took me places that I would otherwise never have gone to, but I do not recall him ever being interested in what I was doing and do not recall him ever praising me for something that I had done. It is not surprising, forgetting every other negative experience I had with him, that the conclusion I arrived at was that he did not care for me, and that, to him, I was unacceptable. I say this with regret and hopefully as a piece of parental advice. Further, though some may find it difficult to believe, I do not hate my father, and have not felt such an emotion for most of my life. I do not say that I never hated my father.

And yet I have been told that, at the time, this was not an unusual practice for parents, that emotion and affection were commonly and quite frequently unexpressed. And if that is true, and I have no reason to doubt it, my father's behaviour towards me was not exceptional. And if that is true then I can only assume that my brothers and sisters had a similar experience of unintentional indifference.

And I could, and indeed would be forced to accept this unconditionally, were it not that my older sister has and had a significantly different perception and experience of my father. With her he seems to have expressed sufficient affection to have generated a view of my father that is vastly different to that of myself, my other brothers and my younger sister.

On the other hand, I find no difficulty in believing this lack of affectional expression was socially widespread, at least among those of their generation. Perhaps parents these days have no difficulty in expressing affection to their children. I suspect this is indeed so. Yet for me, as an individual, I experienced this "indifference" as if it were happening only to me, and learnt self-doubt and a very deep and almost unconscious belief that I should not expect others to love me, as the only reasonable explanation, given the lack of any other believable conclusions for his parental opaqueness.

One does not, after all, with no evidence to the contrary, intuitively believe that one is loved. In other words, if there is no reason to believe that one is loved, there is no reason to so believe. In the absence of such evidence, it is indeed reasonable to conclude that one is not loved. Moreover, I would not be surprised if my other siblings had a similar experience, though each of their experiences would be composed of unique variables that would differentiate each from the other.

In fact, as shown by my older sister's differing experience, there must have been varying degrees of felt rejection and non-valuation in each of us, and to this inner calculation must be added the input by my/our mother, who possessed a quite different personality and set of inner needs.

My parents met at a Sydney radio station, 2UE where they were both working. My mother was employing her university education writing jingles for the station. I have no idea what my father was doing. There is also a story that my mother was getting over an unhappy love relationship when they met. Yet there seems to have been love, at least for some time. In a Book of Common Prayer my mother gave my father at Christmas 1940, she writes: "To my dearest Fred, God bless you always". If only that love had continued a while longer, and what was the cause of its loss!? At the end of my father's life, after they had separated, he told me that he still loved my mother. How much suffering this world has known.

Many was the time
my mother protected me
from my father's rage
when I was young,
translated my Latin set pieces,
lifted her blankets to let me lie
beside her in the morning.
Yet as she lies in hospital
old and worn out,
her heart barely beating,
lungs full of fluid
and close to death,
I feel no tears
no cry of loss.
Like a calm lake
my heart lies silent,
still,
unseemingly unmoved by her suffering
as she never was
to mine.

It's not an old woman's face
I see.
Looking down at my dying mother
on the hospital bed.
Closing my eyes
I see her young,
poring over Roman law
as she thinks of her future,
of the ski trip to Kosciusko,
the job she will get
and the man she will marry,
... full of life and hope
and strength.
The face behind these tired eyes

and wrinkled skin,
is young still,
despite the years,
and time
that betrayed young dreams.

At 9:25 I was told
the unthinkable.
And all day
I have struggled with the news,
sought to unravel
the problem
that was no problem,
take hold of the question that lay
somewhere beyond the horizon
of my thoughts
because I thought I knew the answer
to this new reality...
only to discover that the answer
to my unrest,
the absence of my sense of loss,
was all the time a question.
Why was I not in tears
at the death of my only
mother ?

Now she is dead.
Gone,
though I long took her for granted,
when she was alive,
and acted kindly
only out of reason,
that this was the way to act
towards a mother.
Now,

no matter where I search,
she will not be there,
and though I call her name
she will not answer,
whatever my feelings towards her
really were.

Additionally, our father, who was dominant in each of our lives, had his own set of needs, "demons" which determined to a great degree how he acted towards each of his children who had their own personalities and therefore brought out either good or less than wonderful behaviours in him.

Thus, though the dominant cultural behaviour was not to express emotions and affection, this social value was not one dimensional in relation to my father's interactions with his children, and even if it had been, the negative impact of this behaviour was experienced as if it were directed only to oneself, for behaviour affects people as solitary individuals. Moreover, I doubt that either of my younger brothers and sister would agree that this cultural norm adequately explains our father's behaviour to each of us.

Father
how sad I feel for you
captured on this photograph
holding the hand of the brother
your mother blamed you
all your life
for killing.
How young you look,
how small and open to hurt,
with one hand on your little brother's shoulder
and the other holding his.
I see you both
standing in an open field,

> who knows where,
> but I recognize you father,
> see the face I knew as 'dad',
> the angry, the drunk, the irrational,
> the unpredictable, the caring.
> How sad your life
> because of him, father,
> and how sad my life
> because of you.

I realize that this poem may cause some to see this as self-pity. I have no defense against this understanding other than the simple truth of the matter. Anyway, putting such reflections to one side, looking back over my young life up to this point I see that though I had discovered I was relatively smart, my one recurring behaviour was that I never thought about what I was doing, or reacted to much of what was happening around me … and never knew, or even thought about, what I wanted from life.

The Extended Family

Both of my parents came from small families. In my father's case there was a younger brother who had died after a tragic accident when my father and he were both very young children. My mother had one younger brother, born in 1915, two years younger than my father, whom I saw only two or three times when I was growing up. There must have been a reason my mother and her brother appeared to have no strong wish to have a close connection in their adult lives, but the result has been that my family has almost no relationship with the only cousins we have, along with their respective families.

My cousin tells me that our families did not meet frequently because her parents strongly disliked my father. Yet this does not seem an adequate explanation. Even if they had hated my father, if my mother and her brother had had a strong and close relationship we would have almost certainly seen more of my uncle and his family, and I, at least, would have some explanation of this problem.

Indeed, my aunt, the wife of my mother's brother, has an almost ghost-like reality, which, in reality, means none. Before my uncle died I visited him and two of his children and their families in Hawke's Bay, on the North Island of New Zealand. He was quite old at this time and I had not seen him for perhaps thirty or more years. Nor had I seen my cousins for all this time. We had a friendly visit and I felt that had it been possible I would have really enjoyed knowing these people, that we had a lot in common. He died a couple of years after this visit, the last of our Mohicans.

Walking along the path
from the old Macquarie lighthouse
to the Gap
grandmother introduced me to
a million years ago,
I see the huge table
of sandstone blocks
that fell outwards,
I suspect,
even before Philip decided to sail
between the Heads
to prepare for my family's arrival
sixty years later.
The waves crash monotonously
on the rocks below
reassuringly,
sending spray high into the air
while the Pacific
rolls out sleepily,
a warm blue carpet

as far as the eye can see.
Along the path
I discovered,
this last time,
the gun emplacements
from my father's war.
My uncle,
the last of our Mohicans,
commanded these guns,
now only enigmatic
circles of cement.
The memories wash over me
as well,
sadly
with none of the reality
of the waves below.
All I knew
are dead that gave this place
a life for me.
Dual citizenship
does not give you back
dead parents, grandparents
and old houses
filled with memories
and mystery.
A hundred years or so ago
the Dunbar
thinking, perhaps,
the Gap was the entrance
between the heads,
crashed here
with massive loss of life.
In some more serious sense
they too had thought
that they were coming home.

Fortunately, my father had numerous aunts and uncles, and though I cannot speak for my brothers and sisters, these became *my* uncles and aunts. Even several of these aunts and uncles "provided" by my father were not known for their social abilities, and of course, they died with the generation of my grandparents. I am aware of five "great" uncles and aunts on my father's side but I feel there may have been more. There may also have been a host of other relatives on my father's mother's side, but once again, as a family we had no contact with them either. Nor did my father ever mention his mother's relatives let alone visit them.

What I find amazing is that there was no real effort, or even interest by anyone for any of us to meet and get to know those to whom we were related. Each person had a constellation of relatives with whom they mixed, yet there seems to have been absolutely no desire to bring these alternate universes together.

On the other hand, these "great" relatives we did know were all an interesting bunch and gave me at least some sense of "my" family. My father's father was an extremely gentle man and we always thought he was rather weak, and totally controlled by my grandmother. As I have grown older and discovered more about my grandfather I discover there was much more to the man, and that in his younger days he had been a man of considerable skill and courage.

His father, my great grandfather, Frederick Charles Sigismund, when he was not at his "real" job with the Maritime Services Board, was a sailor all his life, and my grandfather had followed in his footsteps. In 1910 my grandfather was a crew-member on the Culwulla 3, one *of* the most famous yachts in the history of the Royal Prince Alfred Yacht Club, sailing from Sydney to Hobart through fierce storms to bring the yacht to race in the Sayonara Cup.

It could well have been the gentleness in my grandfather, a gentleness my great, great grandfather, Robert Dudley Sidney Powys Herbert (Robert Dudley Adams) saw in him and tried to protect, that my father believed he saw in me, a gentleness or reticence he hated. As he observed my grandfather interacting with my grandmother, and saw him repeatedly submit to her, he may have come to despise what he saw as weakness in my grandfather. He may have watched as my grandmother put the blame for his brother's death on my father and never heard my grandfather speak up to defend my father against her accusations, and so came to resent his father, and despise what he saw as terrible, and almost unforgivable.

Consequently, he may have been reminded of this when he saw any gentleness in me. I say there was gentleness in me, not because I saw, or remember this in myself, I remember nothing, but because that is what I have been told by my family. In finding his son unacceptable, my father may well have been unconsciously responding to the hurt and anger he had experienced from the inability or unwillingness of his father to defend him as a child. And yet, that is exactly how my father acted in regards to me, though this was not in response to my mother.

My father always denied that he had been held responsible for his brother's death but the human mind can learn to blot out from consciousness that which is unbearable. Moreover, relatives tell that my father as a young man felt a deep guilt and responsibility for his brother's death. Almost certainly this guilt had been sown in his heart by his mother, probably as a way to deal with her own feelings of guilt at failing to seek medical help until it was too late, and yet when my father's brother died my father could have been no more than eleven or twelve years old. It is unbelievably sad, but it is not surprising that my father could not recall being blamed for his brother's death. I can remember so much of my life, and yet I have almost no memory of my father's dealings with me. And something must explain my father's "demons".

My great grandfather, who died on the 6th July, 1938, was one of the original members of the RPAYC and sailed competitively all his life. His love of the yacht club found its final expression in his wish to have his ashes sprinkled around a group of trees he and other founders had planted years before at the opening of the yacht club's new grounds at Pittwater.

What other activities my grandfather was involved in in the club I have not discovered, but his father must have had a deep relationship with other members, as in 1897 my great grandfather was friends with Moffat Marks, the owner of the Culwulla 3 that, in 1910, my grandfather sailed down to Hobart.

Frederick Sigismund was my father's grandfather. He may even have known my great great grandfather, Robert Dudley. He must, at least, have heard stories about his great grandfather whose life was filled with mystery, tales of a lost heritage, and perhaps mythology. He could have told us stories about his "ancestors", and I suppose if I had had any curiosity, I could have asked him to tell me these family tales. Partly, my own personality and deep hatred of my father rather made this need for conversation impossible. If only I had asked. Indeed, there were so many people I could have spoken to: Aunt Ruby, uncle Harold, my grandfather, both of my grandmothers. What a waste of memories I did not even consider. My mother's strong dislike of the Adams family tale of lost glory may have also made my father reticent about raising the issue with his children.

My grandfather had at least two sisters and my memory of them is of two elderly unmarried women, dressed in black, wearing heavy diamond earrings that had, over the years, pulled the lobes of their ears down, with delicate lace veils shading their faces. I saw one of these aunts, Ann, rarely, but we frequently visited the other, aunt Ruby in her flat on Billyard Avenue in Elizabeth Bay.

As I grew up I visited this aunt whenever I was in Sydney. She had never married and had been the travelling companion to one of the Bowden family related to Charlotte Louisa (Bowden) Adams, my great grandmother. Charlotte, whose father had been lost at sea, was under age when she married and needed the permission of her mother to marry. At the moment I am looking at a framed medical bill dated 27th, January 1916. It does not tell who the patient was but Charlotte died around this time following a gall bladder operation, so it is likely that this is the bill for the operation that killed her.

Apparently my great aunt had sung opera, and after the First World War had travelled around Europe and England as the companion of the wife of this somewhat distant relative who later gave my aunt, Charlotte's daughter, an inheritance so that she could live securely into her old age.

This distant relative may, in fact, have been Charlotte Louisa (Bowden) Adams' brother, Charles Bowden, as I have an old photograph dated La Conner, Washington state, March, 25, 1889 of his steam schooner entering La Conner Harbour, and addressed to his brother in law Fred Adams, my great grandfather. Moreover, I have another photo of himself and his two daughters, dated August 15, 1896, America taken at a photographer's studio in Seattle. Both of the daughters are almost the spitting image of my younger sister and Charles closely resembles my uncle Harold, Charlotte's son. Charles could well have been the one who provided for my aunt, perhaps following the early death of his sister, my great grandmother.

In a nation that vigorously asserts each person's equality, Aunt Ruby had a servant, Marna, who appears to have also been her companion in her old age. It was in her flat that I first saw television. I can still recall the absolutely magical feeling of watching a game of cricket on her tiny black and white TV. If only such a pure feeling of wonder had continued. In her dining room there was a large round mahogany table that she had apparently bought in China, and in the living room, an ivory statue that, because of its beauty, left a permanent mark on my sense of what was beautiful. Her ivory statue was certainly my motivation for buying an ivory statue in India when I was there briefly. I believe now that ivory should not be traded but, with some guilty pleasure, I am happy and relieved I was able to buy this before the purchase of such items became illegal.

My grandfather had, at least two brothers. One I visited with my father, just once, named Bob after my great, great grandfather, the first member of our family to settle in Australia. His house was on the water in Sydney harbour and he had a yacht tied up at the bottom of his yard. Though apart from this I do not remember him at all, it appears he was in the Boer War and was shot, the bullet going through one of his eyes. The story passed on to me was that he would have died if the Boers had not cared for him.

His other brother, the youngest of my grandfather's brothers and sisters, named Harold, we knew well and used to visit whenever we were in Sydney. At one time in his young life my father had lived with him and his wife. Though brought up Church of England he had converted to Judaism when he married my aunt. Almost certainly it was through him that my father was given a job in a Jewish newspaper, and he certainly looked Jewish, until they discovered my father was not Jewish. This uncle was very successful, and rose to be the Managing Director of the Manufacturers Mutual Insurance Company. This was not the reason we visited him, but there was almost certainly an element of pride in the knowledge of what he was.

Each year, even after he retired, he would be given a new, very large, Mercedes and I remember being picked up by him and driven to various places. I loved this man, and after I left home I would make a point of visiting him. I remember once when I was driving home to Brisbane from Adelaide and not wanting to bother him and his wife I bought a couple of pork chops to be cooked at his house. In total innocence, or perhaps insensitivity, I told him I had these and asked if it would be pos-sible to cook them. Very kindly he reminded me that they were Jewish, and then went and had them cooked for me.

He was very kind to me and once drove into the Army base at South Head, one of the entrances to Sydney Harbour, so that I could see the chapel that was on the base. On another occasion, thinking I was late to catch my plane he drove his large Mercedes along the shoulder of the packed highway to the airport at a fair speed, telling me that he was not worried about being stopped because he knew powerful people. He was a very contradictory person, but over the years he helped both my grandfather and my father get established in business. Years later, my uncle was killed by a bus while he was crossing a street, not the way for anyone to die.

My father's mother, who had been a McWade/Waide/Qaide, was a tiny woman with a very strong personality and lived to be 93. I was quite pleased that none of my ancestors had been convicts until I was informed that her grandfather, or possibly her great grandfather, had been a convict for 13 years in Van Diemen's Land, later called Tasmania. This had been one of the cruellest prisons in pre-federation Australia and he had been sent out from Ireland for an undiscovered crime. In Ireland he had been married, but once one got to Australia there was almost no going back, and after he was given his freedom he had married again, going into business in northern Tasmania. After he had been freed, his daughter from his earlier marriage in Ireland came out to Australia. Had she remembered this man as her father back in Ireland, and had come out to be with him? Had she been upset that he had remarried, and had her father, hardened by his convict experiences, reacted to her lack of acceptance or unhappiness at his new wife, with anger and, in effect, driven her away? Whatever the reasons, the reunion ended badly. For me, this information was rather humbling, though many Australians these days are quite proud of their convict forbears. It is doubtful they would be similarly proud of any contemporary relatives if they were in a similar situation.

During many Christmases my family would drive down to Sydney for the holidays and have Christmas lunch with my father's parents at their cake shop in an apartment above the store. The shop was registered only to my grandmother, not to both my grandparents. This may suggest something. My grandfather's name was Willoughby and their store was on Willoughby Road in the suburb of Willoughby, an interesting fact with clearly no great significance.

Of course the store was closed on Christmas day, and my father would whistle a few bars of a particular tune and we would be let into their "house", walk through the cake shop past a long counter and a large mixing machine, and go up some stairs into their apartment. The upstairs was crammed with furniture and other personal things but my grandmother was a cook, and we would happily eat Christmas lunch around their overcrowded dining room. They had a cut glass bottle of carbonated water that was filled with gas from a small metal bottle that was connected to the cut glass bottle. To a small boy this was an amazing creation.

When my grandparents retired they sold this business and moved back to Katoomba in the Blue Mountains where my father had grown up. Here they bought a duplex on Cascade Street just off the main Katoomba Street that led down to the Three Sisters, living in one half and renting the other to a very nice middle-aged Jewish woman who had previously lived in Malaya.

It was here that we stayed when we visited my father's family, and the cake shop became a distant memory. My grandmother always looked after me when I visited but I do not recall her ever taking me anywhere or talking to me about either her life, or mine.

The contrast between my grandparent's lifestyle and that of the rest of my grandfather's family is stark, and I can only wonder at the thoughts he must have had as he remembered his younger and more exciting years. I suspect he was not born for this world, and was never able or willing to struggle against

the current and make something of himself. Indeed, he may not
have even known how.

The Katoomba House
It was not a very pretty house
The place my father came back to
and breathed his last
in the town where he had
never finished school, grown up,
and suffered
Been cast out twice
Once by his mother and once by mine.
The mountains are
Mysterious, even dangerous
Where they lived.
The unseen valleys fill with fog
And streets are silenced in the clouds
people vanish in the mist
cars creep carefully
Up and down the hills
And rock faces
That have held a million years,
with monstrous crash
And terrifying roar,
Fall far below to the valley floor.
We went there almost every year
When I was growing up.
I'd go to Echo point,
Afraid to look down
into empty space to the valley beneath
And, past the Three Sisters,
climb down the thousand steps
Carved from the rock
To the gum trees, and the by gone
Coal mine in the cliff.

And just for those who'd know
I'm sure that no one else would care
We'd climb the pilgrim pathway
To the Paragon,
An art deco rest stop,
Dance rooms once crowded, empty now
dark... waiting....
For Napoleons, and Devonshire tea
A long held family rite.
My father's grave in rocky soil
Is in the family plot. I try to find it,
Sometimes can't.
We sold the house where Dad had died,
His mother sometime later,
Alone.
I wasn't told. I didn't go
and do not know
if any others from the family
took the time.

After my grandmother died, my wife and I, on a trip from Canada, decided to clean up the empty house and overgrown yard so that my brothers and sisters and I could sell the house. It turned out to be backbreaking work and though we could sleep in the house it was the middle of winter, and without heaters the house was freezing. We decided to rent a caravan in the caravan park nearby, and so finally were able to get a warm night's sleep.

I cannot remember if we found anything of even a little value in the house. Other relatives had gone through things and there really wasn't much more than garbage. We put the house on the market and it was, of course, eventually sold, but this is one more case where we should have kept it, rented it out and sold when prices went up, which they did, considerably. A lesson, but I have no idea if my other brothers and sisters would have been willing to wait. None of us had any experience of real estate at that time.

To talk about my mother's parents is to enter a different world entirely. They lived in Bellevue Hill, and from their back veranda one could see from the beginning of Bondi Junction on the left, to the southern edge of the Sydney Harbour Bridge and the water. Across the valley that dropped off from their house was a church. It may have been All Saints Woolhara where all, I believe, of my sisters and brothers, including my youngest brother, were baptized. This church, whether it was All Saints or not, at various times throughout the day would ring an extremely lovely Carillion bell set.

I do not need to describe my grandparents' house. I have done this elsewhere. In 1917 they moved to Bellevue Hill from Hurstville, a suburb to the south, where both my mother and uncle were born, when my mother was seven years old. At the time, Bellevue Hill was still quite undeveloped. My uncle remembers seeing rabbits running around on the paddocks surrounding the Bellevue Hill house and my grandfather trying to shoot one using my uncle's Daisy air gun, a rather optimistic possibility at best. Having grown up after the suburb became completely developed and "civilized" it is difficult to imagine such a pastoral scene, but this accords with my grandmother's relating to me as a very young child that there was a dairy nearby where I imagine they bought their milk. Pedlars would lead their horses around the area selling their goods and my grandparents once bought some goldfish that they put into a square stone pond at the bottom of their fernhouse, from one of these tradesmen.

What it was I do not know, but apparently my grandparents did a favour for a young artist, Elioth Gruner. I wonder, sometimes, if the nearby dairy was the location of one of Gruner's famous paintings. I also wonder if my grandmother mentioned the dairy to me as an unconscious inner allusion to Gruner's painting and the favour, whatever it was, she had done for the artist. Perhaps they allowed him to stay in their house while he painted local scenes.

In appreciation for this unknown favour, the artist painted a picture for them as a gift. An artist does not paint a 3 foot by 2 foot painting for the gift of a cup of tea. My grandparents must have done something quite significant to be given a painting in "payment", and I doubt that they gave him money.

In excessive humility, one hopes, they told him he did not need to sign it. The fact that they told him he needn't sign it is almost an acknowledgement that they saw him as either a potentially famous painter or one who already was one, and that they were aware of the economic or social value of the signature, and that this awareness, for some reason, troubled them. Perhaps they were ashamed or embarrassed by the feelings or thoughts it generated in them. Years later it took some time to authenticate the painting as a genuine Gruner. After my grandmother died, my uncle donated this painting to the Armidale Presbyterian Ladies College.

That is the story I grew up with. However, my cousins inform me that there is much that is incorrect in my rendition. What they believe to be true is that Elioth Gruner, who had been living in his mother's house in Carr's Wood, painted the "Greet" painting, titled " A Summer's Day", in 1910 in Carr's Wood Park near Botany Bay, a year before my mother was born. Furthermore, the artist was living with his mother at this time, which limits the possibility that my grandparents did the artist a favor. Moreover, the painting had not been donated to the Armidale Presbyterian Ladies' College as I had incorrectly believed, but rather to the Armidale Teacher's College.

In a perfect example of a failure to tell family stories, the Teacher's College had actually been suggested to my uncle for the donation by my mother, who had heard they had a collection of about fifteen Gruner paintings. There is newspaper evidence to support this alternate narrative, which I can only accept.

According to the Greet family, my grandfather, a close neighbour of the Gruners, was a friend of the artist, who gave the painting to him as a gift. So where did I get the story of the 'favour'? My cousins' information does not explain why the gift was given, though they add much narrative detail. They also do not explain why the painting was not signed. A great deal of what I believed to be true is clearly incorrect. Nevertheless, could the essence of the two narratives be complementary? If nothing else, it raises the fascinating question of both how family histories are generated, and the degree to which they should sometimes be only tentatively accepted.

I do not remember my grandfather at all. He died after an asthma attack when I was very young, perhaps seven or eight, though that in itself should not mean I do not remember him. Apparently, he was fond of my older sister, who has affectionate memories of him. I wish I did remember the man for he and my grandmother had a holiday house about sixty miles north of Sydney at a tiny whistle stop named Tascott which was really the combination of the name of one of the area's important people, T.A. Scott, perhaps the first man to bring sugarcane to New South Wales. The grandson of T.A. Scott lived in the house next to my grandparent's cottage and it was he who befriended my grandfather and taught him what tackle he needed and where to catch fish, as up to that time he and my uncle had been patently unsuccessful in this venture. After this unusual act of unselfishness my uncle relates that they always came home with a basket full of fish.

My parents usually drove to Tascott, but occasionally we travelled by train. As the train slowly wound its way along parts of the track that were being repaired, the railway workers would cry out "papers, any newspapers". They must have had to spend the nights along the track and either had no way of getting to a store for the news or were bored and simply had nothing to do in their spare time.

The house was surrounded by bush and I remember a beautiful moth about two or three inches across that I saw onetime on the wall of the outside toilet. I have been told, and given the surrounding bush it may well be true, that I also saw a lyrebird once, though I have no recollection of this. There were three or four Aboriginal or New Guinea native spears displayed in one corner of the living room and each bedroom had a large bowl and pouring vessel that were common in houses before the time of running water.

Tascott.
Among the trees
along the lonely Hawkesbury shores,
grandfather's wood frame weekend house,
one of four or five
from which the whistle stop of a station
had got its name.
Down the dirt, two rut path,
past cotton flower pods
that popped mysteriously under foot,
between walls of high grass
and the long railway fence
that kept us from crossing straight to the water,
we walked
undemanding,
untied
and tied the wooden railway gate
yet again.
Across the tracks we'd amble down
the narrow pot-holed road
that stretched beside the shore.
There were no cars,
or one or two,
no need to look or worry
about a lunatic driver

or some sick soul out to harm seven year olds
as we made our way
down to the narrow old wharf
with the rotting wooden swimming pool,
that never looked the place to swim.
The smell of salt and drying seaweed
filled the air.
Gentle waves brushed the stony beach
and, somehow.... out of place,
a huge rock sat beside the shore,
washed by the tide.
The Gosford train, gleaming green,
rushed past each day,
letting out its eerie cry
and leaving in its wake
the sweet smell of burnt coal.
It's good grandfather died.
The fish have gone
from where he used to catch
great jew and flathead every time,
the dusty tracks that led unhurried
to the railway gate,
the wooden pool gone too.
Along the Hawkesbury's shores
a four laned highway feeds the hills
clear now of nought but trees.
Washed by the tide
the rock alone remains.

I remember being in this house many times so he must have been there also. I can only assume he had minimal contact with me. I remember him as a fisherman who had a small motorboat tied up to a narrow wooden wharf down on the water that the house looked out on. Why I remember the house clearly, the little wharf, and the path down to the jetty but not my grandfather, troubles me, and I wish he had spent more time with me, for my grandmother, though, it seems she had been very "hard" on my mother when she was growing up, is a lovely memory, and one of the most important people in my life.

The fact that my older sister has an extremely different view of my father to all the rest of my family, and that she has a similarly pleasant and affectionate memory of my grandfather almost angers me. Not that they acted differently and more favourably to her, but that the power of gender attraction, (along the lines that boys relate to their mothers and girls to their fathers), creates such differing memories and perceptions of personality, and has such an effect on a child's personality development.

I have my grandfather's Book of Common Prayer given to him by his godmother on the 27th of March, 1889 on his fifth birthday. In contrast, I was given a prayer book at my baptism and being given a prayer book on his 5th birthday suggests that the infant mortality rate at that time was quite high or perhaps, that the cultural rituals that sprang from this sad state were still prevalent, and the family, possibly without even thinking about it, waited to see if my grandfather survived until, at least, this young age, which was twenty two years before the birth of my mother in 1911.

He was a Director of E Way and Co. Ltd, a large department store in Sydney where he worked from 1907 till 1951 when he retired, and was also active in a militia where he won awards for shooting and, unsurprisingly, trained soldiers to shoot in World War 2. However, fortunately for my grandfather, because of his asthma he was never involved in World War 1. My cousins, on the other hand, believe that the reason for this was his curvature of the spine. It could be that both of these maladies are correct.

My grandfather, Harold Trevanion, was born in Hammersmith, Middlesex county, in London, on the 27th of March, 1884, although most of his family ancestors were born in Torpoint, in Cornwall (which seems to explain why my grandparent's house in Bellevue Hill was so named) and migrated to Australia, arriving here in 1902, the day of his 18th birthday.

His father, Thomas Greet, on the other hand, was born in 1854 in Torpoint and, for some reason, must have felt a need to travel all across southern England to London. According to police records, he joined the London police force in 1872, when he was eighteen, and was appointed a detective inspector in 1889. An amusing addendum to this apparent paragon of probity is that the police record notes that he had a tattoo on his left wrist.

Nevertheless, what, to me, is fascinating and thought provoking, is that my grandfather, not quite eighteen years old, his eldest child, and as far as I know his only son, migrated to Australia (on the other side of the world) just a year after his father retired. And neither my cousins nor I have ever heard why he undertook this apparently permanent uprooting journey. My mother seems to have told one of my sisters that he joked that it was to escape his sisters. This, however, does not seem entirely believable. There surely must have been some affection for them as my mother was named Arnold after her maternal grandmother and Glennie after one of his sisters.

I am also not aware that he moved to Australia with any other relative, nor have I ever heard that he returned to Britain, even once, to visit. And how did he react when he was told his father had died, for surely he was informed of this? It was certainly not that he hated or even disliked Britain. My grandparents' house was replete with quite large pictures of British military and naval power and glory, although, surprisingly, I do not recall any scenes of the English countryside. Indeed oddly, in one of the lounges, surrounded by this array of British glory, there was one fairly large picture of a North American Indian in a canoe paddling along a dark wooded waterway, that did not go with any other picture in the house. If one's pictures reflect the inner person, what was this one trying to tell us? Perhaps he did not wish to be reminded, or was it that he was more like his policeman father than he was aware, while yet disliking this possibility? Perhaps he moved to Australia to escape his father.

A Knife and Fork.
I cut into the pear's flesh
pry out the seeds inside
the special fork and knife
grandfather used
in the dining room,
in his leather chair
beside the fire
below the picture of George V
listening to the news
on 2UE.
I cut up the pear
each pear
each time remembering
my long dead grandfather
Harold Trevanian Greet
from England
my mother's father
my dead mother's father,
while my daughter
sits in the next room
watching TV.

My grandmother was born on the 3rd of March, 1881 in Timaru, in the South Island of New Zealand, and told me that as a young teenager she had been sent to a Roman Catholic school in Sydney, even though she was Church of England. This would explain why she would always light a candle when she took me to St Mary's Cathedral. My uncle wrote that my grandmother was born on the 4th of March 1883. However her birth certificate gives a different date approximately 3 years earlier. My grandparents apparently met at either Grace Brothers, the large Sydney department store where they both worked, or at St Barnabas' Anglican church, and married on the 31st of December, 1909, two years after my grandfather moved to E Way and Co., and two years before my mother was born.

Like my father's mother she was a small woman, and after the early death of her husband, also lived almost into her 90's, living until the final two and a half years of her life in the house she and her husband had bought and shaped, years before. Apparently, she had told my grandfather that she was three years younger than she actually was, maybe so that he would not think she was older than he was, or more likely, so he would not realize she was as old as she was, and still unmarried.

During the war, as my father and uncle were in the Armed Forces, my mother and my aunt came to live in my grandparents' house. However, after reading my uncle's account of his wartime military postings (about which I now know more than I do of my own father's) I cannot find that my aunt ever lived in the Bellevue Hill house with my mother. Indeed, he never mentioned that she did. My sister and I, on the other hand, were born nearby in Vaucluse in Clairvaux, a small private hospital that no longer exists, and lived the first few years of our lives in this house.

This being so, the unfriendly view that my mother and my aunt did not get along well in these cramped quarters, a view I had long held, simply cannot be claimed. In fact, though my uncle's family had rather strong negative feelings towards my father, I doubt they felt any such unfriendliness towards my mother.

Later, five or six years after the war, my parents moved six hundred miles north to Brisbane, reputedly to escape both of their respective in-law families and the consequent conflicts resulting from such propinquity. My family would, nevertheless, travel down to Sydney to visit their families during many end of year holiday seasons.

We must have stayed with my grandmother in Bellevue Hill when we came down, for my father's parents had no room in their already overcrowded apartment for any of us. This worked, for my father could take us to uncle Harold's relatively close house in Dover Heights for a visit, and it was within easy driving distance from his house or my grandparents' house to either Bondi beach or Neilson Park. Neilson Park had a shark net placed across the entrance to a small bay where people could safely swim, and even though it was inside the harbour it was a wonderful place to swim, and occasionally had ocean sized waves.

In a cold Calgary room
memories of Sydney Harbour,
yachts,
warm waves,
and the swell of the sea,
lifting, lifting.

On the other hand, I remember swimming in Bondi and being roughly dumped into the sandy bottom by breaking waves. If this has not been one of your experiences, let me tell you it is not part of the fun of swimming in the ocean. I was just a child, and obviously had not learned how to avoid such indignities.

We used to change into our swimming costumes after we got to these places, wrapping a towel around our waists so we could take off our clothing and put on our swimming trunks while surrounded by crowds of sunbathers. Of course there was always the danger that the towel would fall down around your ankles while you were only partly clothed, but it seemed to work.

These trips to Sydney began the practice of sending me, though not every year, to stay with my mother's mother. I remember once being put, by myself, on a DC6 in Brisbane en route to Sydney. There it had been arranged for me to be met, I don't remember by whom, and then driven in a hire car by a one armed veteran of World War 2 that my grandmother knew, to my grandmother's house.

My sister has no memory of this kind of thing happening for her and I think that my mother's motivation may have been to allow me time away from my father. The mere fact that it occurred suggests that the memory I have of my father finding me less than he wished is not far from the truth. I record this only as an objective fact and not as a criticism of my father who "at other times" must have acted in a fatherly manner to me.

Reflecting the nature of most children, I suspect, when I was with my grandmother I did not realize the generosity of her behaviour towards me. She went out of her way to take me to interesting places, once to a pantomime, to nice restaurants in the city, several times to the Gap at the entrance to Sydney Harbour, the Museum, Hyde Park, St Mary's Cathedral, the Botanical Gardens, and the Mitchell Art Gallery. I also remember on at least one occasion, being taken by ferry, almost certainly by my grandmother, across the harbour from Circular Quay to the Taronga Park zoo. After walking up from the ferry wharf we entered the world of animals, Secretary birds, tigers and elephants in too small cages, though no one seemed to understand this at the time, and penguins in the aquarium section. I found none of this boring in any way.

It was on one of these visits that my grandmother took me to visit my uncle and his family in North Sydney, in Castle Crag where they lived, and must have been one of the few times I had any contact with this side of my family.

The Archibald Fountain
We used to walk
down the steep hill
from Bellevue Hill
to Double Bay,
to shop for Neenish tarts,
my grandmother and I.
She must have been
much younger
than I remember her
when I was older,
and strong enough
to walk up and down
steep hills
and the stone steps
of the little winding paths between the streets.
We sometimes
caught the tram
to the city
and the circular track
with the victorious Queen
it slowly clattered
around
disrespectfully disgorging passengers
just outside
Hyde Park
with the fountain
full,
I thought,
of naked female shapes
and mythic bulls that
I could never look at
without fear and
embarrassment
fascinated by their bronze breasts

as I still am.
The reflecting pool before the War Memorial
led across the street
to the Museum
serene and peaceful,
filled with still, safe life,
then to St. Mary's
where we'd light a candle
to a Catholic God
and light shone down
from storied windows high above
into the gloom
and in the quietness
people spoke in whispers
not in fear but wonder and in awe.
At other times
we'd head toward the Harbour
or the Art Gallery.
I've never seen the Louvre
but love the Mitchell
with its giant painting of
Roberts' "Bailed Up",
I bought in a print sale
in London, Ontario
years later
and hung on my wall
to remind me of an earlier life.
Its marble nudes
never filled me with the fear
the other
bronze ones did
glistening wet,
and kneeling on their basalt bases
so close they could almost be
touched.

My grandma always seemed
surrounded
by a peace I never knew
at home.
No fights, no fear
no raised voices
in the high quiet rooms of her
lovely, simple house on the hill.
The only tension
that I ever felt with her
was in my guilty glances
walking near the fountain girls
calling me to a world
at twelve, and even twenty
they
and she
could never take me.

* Note 1: there is only one, not particularly voluptuous nude female sculpture in this fountain.

* Note 2: It was the Roberts of this famous painting who caused a great deal of trouble to my great great grandfather in the later part of the nineteenth century. It appears Roberts, who at this time had risen from poverty into the upper classes of Sydney, and seems to have lived in Balmain, the same suburb as my great great grandfather, had had a propensity to organize protests against "unfairness" dating from his time as an art student in Melbourne. A picture of these two upper class gentlemen, who almost certainly knew each other, being involved in a public contest against my great great grandfather's semi-complete beginning of a coal mine in North Sydney is fascinating, and probably I would have to take the side of Tom Roberts. His protest and litigation certainly had an economic impact on my family's 'state', and may have led to RDA's and his children's remaining in the colony.

As just remarked, in the late eighteen hundreds, my great great grandfather, Robert Dudley, was one of a company attempting to mine coal. The area was clearly not very developed residentially at the time, but perhaps it was beginning to be. Tom Roberts was one of the leaders of a group, who today would probably be called environmentalists, and who strongly opposed this mining proposal.

Robert Dudley and company seem to have begun the mining operation without a complete environmental examination of its impacts (at least that is how it would be described today). After a great deal of protest and litigation the mining was halted, and my great great grandfather almost certainly lost a great deal of money. I suspect, given his company's lack of a thorough preparation, that he was not a very good businessman.

My grandmother and I would also walk down the hill to the vegetable shop, or the butcher shop, at the bottom of Kambala Road, or further down the hill to Double Bay, along the shady tree-lined streets around her house, down the little pathways between the streets, and to Cranbrook College, a famous college nearby. Many of these streets had fascinating names, Bulkara, Kambala and Ginahgulla, that sound Aboriginal, and I would be told information about what we were walking by, such as that the little building at the entrance to such and such a house had, at one time been the carriage house where the coach driver had lived.

In her kitchen my grandmother, in the early days of our visits, had an icebox instead of a refrigerator, which, nevertheless, she did later acquire, so that each week a large block of ice about 20 inches by 1 foot and about 10 inches thick would be delivered to replace the one that had almost melted. Beside this was a high walk-in pantry with shelving along all three sides. On the inside of its door were written measurements telling the heights of all her grandchildren, as they progressively grew taller.

Granny was a wonderful cook and would make delicious lemon cheese tarts, and in the mornings, give us slices of white bread, toasted on the green enamelled tray she would slide into the opening under the "toast making" element of her gas stove and cut up into four fingers that my sister and I thought was the only correct way to eat toast.

Each day, in the morning and evening, she would take breadcrumbs to the front lawn for the birds, some of which were particularly pretty. Around the front yard of her house, near where she fed the birds, we would sometimes find the discarded "shells" of cicadas that had crawled out of these shells and become large green and rusty coloured but noisy flying insects, and inside the house, in one corner of the lounge, being looked after for one of his friends by my uncle, stood a large, many drawed collection of multi-sized bird's eggs, that included, an enormous emu egg,

About three houses down from her house lived the Dyes, a family she had known from the earliest days of Bellevue Hill and who also had a holiday house in Tascott, though I do not recall ever going to it. Mr. Dye had been a carpenter in a very primitive New Guinea when he was younger. Indeed, it may have been he who gave my grandparents the spears that were in their Tascott house. *He* and his wife were kind friends to us as young children and even as adults, who used to visit from my grandparents' house up the road.

Kambala Road.

When I was one,
a time of war,
I lived in Bellevue Hill.
Each year I would return
to grandma's house
see Napoleon's retreat,
and the British fighting square

blood stained in glorious red
defending the flag
in the dim hall
between high ceilinged rooms,
and in the lounge,
Napoleon on the Bellerophon
sailing into exile on St Helena,
and huge dark Dreadnoughts
cutting through surging waves
on a moonless cloud-filled night,
climb down the stone steps
to the square goldfish pool
at the bottom of the fernhouse
and count the agapanthus
that filled the ridge beside the house.
Each morning
I'd watch her on the lawn
just beyond the red-tiled verandah,
outside the room she had
in happy by gone days, once shared,
drop bread crumbs on the grass
for birds,
bul-buls, sparrows and blue wrens,
and at night I'd hear the fire trees rustle
mysteriously against the wall
as I lay in thickly quilted comfort
alone in the room
where once my mother slept,
beside my grandmother's.
When grandma died
they tore down the house,
broke down the fernhouse
and the goldfish pool,
filled in the spaces of my memories
with white plaster,

built a new fence,
and locked me out.

When my grandmother died my mother and my uncle inherited the house. There were many things in the house that she could have asked for, yet she chose almost nothing. Except for one picture, which I have, she apparently wanted nothing, save for a tiny number of items belonging to my grandmother. My sister and I, if no one else, were not asked if we were interested in any of the items in the house, (culture and perhaps the emotion of the division crowded out any others that my mother and her brother who, in a more calm situation, would have remembered) and I have no idea what happened to them. I suspect some, perhaps all of the pictures, large and small, were taken by my uncle. In fact I have heard two stories about the fate of the pictures in Bellevue Hill. One is that they were given to the Armidale University, a story I have doubts about, as most of the large pictures were not, as I remember them, original paintings. The other is that my uncle did, in fact get these, but that they were damaged by water in storage. Either may be correct but, frankly, the second seems more likely. I am fairly sure that had my mother asked for anything my uncle would have unhesitatingly agreed. My mother could have kept some. She chose to leave the majority of my grandparents' things for my uncle.

Had she felt for so long that she had been grievously *and unfairly treated by both of her parents, in favor of her brother* for much of her life? Is this why we saw her brother so infrequently? And was this part of a rejection, a turning away from her mother, a final revelation of the anger she seems to have felt for her mother for how she believed she had been treated? If so, it is as sad as the death of the person to whom she was finally expressing her truest feelings.

My grandmother's house was magical, not only to my brothers and sisters and me, but also to my uncle's children, our cousins. In my mind I can walk through every room, walk along every verandah, and none is empty of a memory of what once was there, see my grandmother polishing the large black slate step that led into the house, and beside the ridge of sky blue agapanthus, walk into the trellised fern house with the giant tree ferns and the flowering crimson and blue fuchsia bushes in two or three foot raised gardens on either side of the narrow path leading to the slightly precarious steps to the square stone goldfish pond, lie on the lawn where she fed the birds in the front, and always feel the uncomfortable buffalo grass pricking my skin. I believe their feelings towards the house and my grandmother were quite similar to ours, and when our grandmother died and the house was sold and torn down, I believe they felt as strong a sense of loss as I did, indeed, as I still do. *Sic transit gloria mundi.*

So What About the Sabbath?

Religion meant very little to me before my first year of high school, and even then it had a quite dubious and rather passive influence. As far as I can remember, all my brothers and sisters and I went to the Methodist Sunday school directly across from our shop on Wynnum Road. This particular little wood frame centre of worship was chosen because it was so close, and the only Church of England church nearby was deemed to be too High Church. My family came from Sydney, predominantly Low Church, and with a long history of Protestant belief and custom. The minister of our Methodist church, the Rev. James Heaton, would drive my brother and sisters and me home after church every Sunday in his little Ford Prefect and I have never discovered why we were so singularly selected for this kindness.

As I helped my father deliver newspapers on Sunday mornings, my mother would make sure my Sunday clothes were at the store so that I could change into them and be presentable at church. I remember once, my mother forgot to send my Sunday clothes and I was forced to walk across to Sunday School in my ordinary working clothes. All through that Sunday School class I was dying of shame. Even as a child and young person, when my brothers or I went to town we had to wear a suit and tie. This practice only accentuated my embarrassment.

My religious life went into, at least second gear, when my friend and I went out at the Leighton Ford Crusade at the Milton tennis courts. Each person who went out had a counsellor assigned them and after a short prayer we were given material to read and bible verses to memorize. I find nothing to fault them in this. It was an intelligent preparation that grounded the decision in a minimal biblical and theological set of ideas that would hopefully be conducive to spiritual growth. We were encouraged to find a church where this basic foundation could be built on. However, my friend and I were already going to our delightful Methodist church and so didn't seem to need to search any further.

As I was writing this I suddenly realized, for the first time in my life, that this was perhaps the most crucial event of my entire life. Virtually everything that has happened to me since this, springs from my apparently simple decision to go out at this crusade appeal. Indeed, I cannot imagine what my life would have been like if this had not happened. Becoming a Christian gave me goals, caused me to think about life, and led me to follow paths that had direction and purpose, where before I had none, no ambitions, no understanding of life, nothing but moment to moment *ad hoc* reactions to what was happening, with no overarching plan or purpose, and no beliefs and ideas through which I could understand and interpret behaviours and events. I am overwhelmed.

Unknown to me, and entirely coincidentally, my older sister had also become a Christian through this Billy Graham crusade. However, instead of attending the little Methodist church, she began attending a newly built Baptist church in an adjoining suburb. My sister was so impressed by the pastor of this church, Pastor Humphreys, that I began going there myself. What was different about this man's preaching was that he seemed to have experienced God in some real way. Rather than being solely expositional and historical, his preaching was pastorally centred on how to live a spiritual life in obedience to God in such a way that one could learn to know God as a real person involved in one's life.

Among all the other things for which I am indebted to my sister, being introduced to two of her friends must certainly be included. One of these was an elderly man named Joseph Smith, not to be confused with the Mormon of the same name. Joe was married to Gracie a quiet and unbelievably thin woman, and together they were two of the holiest people I have ever met. They lived simply in a wood frame house that made my parents' house look palatial. He was a cabinetmaker, I believe, and would occasionally be asked to preach in the local Baptist church.

Each Saturday he would visit a hospital for the incurably ill, and go around greeting the patients, staying for a short while with each one. One Saturday he took me with him but with me such visitations did not generate any interest. With him these people were human beings to whom small gifts of compassion could be shared, while I felt no connection. On the other hand he had a daughter, Heather, who I was seriously attracted to, though this was not returned, and understanding my unhappiness at this he told me kindly that in ten years all these problems would be resolved. In my case it took considerably longer. Joe and Gracie's house was a model of what sincere Christianity could be, and a refuge where I could safely ask questions and be accepted.

If Joe Smith was my "father in Israel" Mrs. Russell, an elderly widow, was the "mother". Both of these people not only knew their bibles, even more importantly, they seemed to know God. Many times on the weekend I would pedal my one speed bicycle the fourteen miles from our house down to Wynnum on the coast to visit. I never thought about the distance, though now, in retrospect, I am amazed that without a thought I would expend all this energy to visit this motherly figure and sometimes be fed, for maybe just a couple of hours. Perhaps, with both of these people, I was seeking stable and caring parent figures. That may be partly true. Yet what I was conscious of when I visited was the spiritual guidance they offered and that I sought.

My older sister lived with this woman for a short time and we both attended a tiny nearby church named Bethel. Oddly, I cannot remember how we got to this church each week, though we may have simply caught one of the old buses that travelled Wynnum Road, not quite a highway, which connected the city (downtown) to the relatively distant coastal suburbs. The pastor of this very small church was a young man named Gerald Tidey and what I still remember of his sermons, and I remember nobody else's, was their focus on Christ as the source of our spiritual life. His was truly Christocentric preaching, and I pray that his life has been or was filled with contentment.

As a gangly seventeen year old I fell in love with a girl, around my own age, named Gay Cardinal, who attended this little church, one of a family of girls Cardinal. My sister and I could be regularly found seated around their table for lunch on a Sunday. This kindness did nothing to diminish my affections, but unfortunately nothing to gain their return. Indeed, she exhibited no great interest in me at all until I became a bible college student, whereupon I was surprised to discover she liked me. Unhappily, by that time I had lost interest, but I remember her as very pretty and a wonderful person. To no great pleasure of mine, this "romantic" pattern of non-achievement, or bad timing, I suspect, continued for much of my life, though it does, I suppose, even to me, seem a little strange and funny.

It was also through this church that my sister and I began to be involved in Keswick holiness conventions held, each Easter on Mt. Tambourine about fifty miles from Brisbane. Oddly, it was not that we did these things together but rather that we both did the same things. The Keswick meetings were held in a large metal building, very open to the air and with no floor other than the grass field on which it stood. There was no registration required and as no chaos ensued, apparently none was needed, and one simply gravitated to whatever organization, if any, one supported.

All the groups, usually missionary societies or church groups, had their own simple building scattered over the mountain, with rooms for sleeping, washrooms and a dining room and conducted their own devotional activities aimed at encouraging one's spiritual life. Each Easter a small number of special speakers would address the hundreds of people who attended, with returning missionaries speaking on the Saturday nights, testifying to the guidance and protection of God while on the mission field, preaching on the biblical need for missions and appealing to people to give themselves to missionary work.

Throughout the convention people would go to the front at the end of most meetings to surrender to God and give themselves to seek a deeper walk with God. The preaching was not judgemental but rather informative, pastoral and inspirational. More importantly, most of those who came to these conventions did not come to be entertained or to be told jokes but because they already wanted a deeper walk with and knowledge of God.

Yet, as strange as it may seem, and perhaps it was my fault, perhaps I was not listening carefully enough, though the speakers were effective in encouraging people to surrender their lives to God, I never understood from what was said how a believer actually grew into a holy person. In most people there, including myself, there was a level of holiness and love for God, though how that was achieved I did not know.

To refer to a bible verse in Jeremiah I am now familiar with, how was the Law of God to be written on my heart? Even though the book of Romans, particularly chapters 6, 7 and 8, the chapters on victory over sin, was often referred to, and the texts were quoted, the meaning of the texts as guides to a holy life never came across, at least for me. The desire for holiness is not in itself sufficient to produce the holiness that is longed for.

I do not remember if I was in first or second year of high school when my religious behaviour increased, but some time then, some students came back from a camp with the message that we Christians needed to communicate with those who did not believe, in order for them to enter into a relationship with God as sons and daughters. In other words, we needed to witness to the lost.

Probably I lack imagination, for I am sure that I was reading the bible on a fairly regular basis. However, the command to spread the Gospel never struck me as involving something I should actively be engaged in. Once I was told that I should be doing this, my life changed.

The first thing I did was to go to the Evangelical bookstore on Queen Street in the city and buy a number of different gospel tracts to hand out. I continued this practice until I left high school. However, while I was in the bookstore I discovered a trove of Christian biographies, biblical commentaries and books on spiritual subjects. This had a powerful impact on my thinking and produced a desire to serve the Lord in some kind of ministry. But what?

Sometime in this search I prayed that God would show me whether I should be a minister or a missionary. The night after I prayed, in fact the very same day, I read Romans 10 in which these words appeared as guidance regarding this prayer: "How shall they hear unless they have a preacher and how shall they preach unless they are sent". I immediately understood this to mean that I should become a missionary. However, this has never happened, and I have never felt that I should have done something that would bring this particular end about.

I may have been wrong to think this was guidance. On the other hand fulfillment of God's directions is sometimes very different to the way they are initially understood. At the very worst, what I thought was direction may not have been so at all, simply coincidence. As it is I became neither a minister nor a missionary. The truth of the text remains, but clearly not all are chosen to be full time religious workers. Moreover, the text does not appeal to all, and so, on one level, it cannot be interpreted as a blanket call to full time ministry, as we usually understand this term.

It was, nevertheless, with this understanding of what I should do with my life that I applied for and was accepted into Bible College. At the time I applied, just a little before this, in fact, I became Pentecostal. The consequence of this was that I chose to attend an Assemblies of God Pentecostal college in Brisbane, situated, appropriately, in Graceville and on the bank of the Brisbane River.

Several years later a flood covered the college, causing the church leaders, no doubt, to reflect on the wisdom of their decision to build it there. Personally, I believe they misunderstood the significance of the flood and moved, for where they moved to provided very little opportunity for the students to gain ministry experience. Ultimately the entire bible college philosophy was abandoned for a university model, and the spiritual aspect of college life was, even if unintentionally, abandoned. The consequence has been, I would argue from the result, a Pentecostal clergy that has a tenuous connection to both pentecostsal teaching and experience. Indeed, the large downtown church many students used to attend, Glad Tidings Tabernacle, affectionately called the Tab, built as a result of a revival and seating several hundred, has now been demolished, the result of continually dwindling numbers and a leadership that increasingly failed to be genuinely Pentecostal.

My brother in law, who was a genuine man of God, was part
of a Russian community that had settled in China after fleeing
a Stalinist Soviet Union. Some time after the communists in
China began to take over more and more of this country most,
if not all of the community split into two groups, one going to
South America and the other to Australia. While still in China,
however, there was a prophecy that Australia would be invaded
and that there would be terrible suffering. This troubled my
brother in law immensely.

A short while before I left Australia for Canada I attended
the Glad Tidings Tabernacle, referred to above, and during the
11 o'clock service there was a prophecy, there may, in fact,
have been two related prophecies, foretelling an invasion of
Australia and followed by a time of great suffering. This church
was quite established, and was not 'in the habit' of making
dramatic proclamations. At this time I was not aware of the
prophecy my brother in law had heard in China, and, in fact,
I only recently was made aware of it by my sister, who was
typing up a tape her husband had made.

I have become increasingly concerned about China's economic and military build-up and, as it happened, it came to me
one morning as I was lying in bed thinking, "we are going to
see the fulfillment of the prophecies my sister knew about, and
that I had heard in Australia". This, after fifty years of wondering at the lack of any reason to think these prophecies would
ever be fulfilled. Before I told my sister what I had recently
been thinking, she told me that she had discovered a reference
to the prophecy in China and was deeply disturbed. I then told
her what I had been thinking and we wondered if this coincidence was significant in any way.

I write this so that it may not be concluded that all the ideas
above were fabricated ex post facto, and perhaps, as a result,
the ways of God might be believed in a more biblical manner.
I hope, very much, that I am wrong about all this.

Bible college turned out to be one of the most formative experiences in my life. No situation is uniformly positive but bible college was predominantly so. I started out badly. One of my first experiences as a student revealed my naiveté and produced consequences that continued for the three years I was a student there. In one of my first classes, taught by the Principal, I spoke up and asked how he, as a Christian, could make a certain statement that I obviously found objectionable. I forget what he had said. I also promptly forgot about my remark, but apparently he did not.

It was not that I had a strong desire to oppose authority, in some kind of unconscious dislike of those in power springing from my hatred of my father, in an environment where I felt I could oppose such authority with impunity. Rather, I suspect, my comment to the principal arose from an incomplete understanding of who actually populated the church. In other words, I failed to realize that the people in the church were also human beings who were, at times, far from being free from very human feelings of hurt and anger at being criticized.

Church leadership does not imply perfect holiness, and at least one dimension of holiness is the healing of the heart/soul from the hurt that each of us has received from other damaged, and less than perfectly holy fellow human beings, some of whom happen to be Christians.

I later had a couple of not very serious "run ins" with him but I had no idea he still harboured resentment from our initial "meeting". At the very end of my life in the college he apologized to me and asked for my forgiveness for his negative attitude. I am sure I was so nonplussed at this and that I said nothing memorable in reply. However, at this late date, too late in fact, I appreciate his feeling and wish I could have met him when I was older and slightly wiser.

My only serious, but not bitter thought on his attitude to me, and to this could be added the philosophy of the teacher-coach for the cricket team in elementary school, is that I wish they had taken a more constructive approach, and instead of simply seeing the skills of those, some of whom could already play, and the limitations of the student before them as fixed entities, they had consciously sought to find ways to develop that person into a more rounded player and better person.

At one time I had the use of my mother's small Austin. This car developed a major front axle problem and I certainly did not have the money to repair it. I prayed about this and sometime after, was surprised to discover the Austin no longer appeared to have a problem. I do not know how that happened, and you can make any interpretation of this that satisfies you. Anyway, I was driving the "miracle car?" up the driveway at the college and apparently drove over a canvas tarpaulin. The principal saw this and got me into the office and rebuked me for my thoughtlessness. There was no one else in the office. Later that day some of us were at a local pool swimming and one of the guest lecturers came up to me in the pool and told me that I had gotten into trouble by driving over the tarpaulin. As far as I know, no one had told him this had happened; at the most he may have seen me drive over the object, and once again you may make of this what you will. If you will allow me, I believe God told him, perhaps to strengthen my faith.

One of the many different classes we had covered basic music. Church is a decidedly musical environment and pastors of churches sometimes need to lead choirs and possess a sense of the congregational music they lead. In the course of this, each student was asked to practice leading the class in a hymn, and so eventually my turn came.

As I was singing in this role, other students began to come to the classroom to hear who was singing. They thought I had a beautiful voice. I had no idea I possessed this talent, and I must have inherited it from my father's side of the family. I have discovered that my brother also has a lovely voice. From then on I sang solos, and with groups, in college, at church and in front of hundreds of people as the college "fund" team travelled around Eastern and Southern Australia during the summer college break. This continued until I migrated to Canada where no one knew who I was and I did not tell them I could sing.

There were times in college when a large group of students travelled in the college bus, probably to a church to minister, and they would spontaneously begin singing a chorus or a hymn. I could not join in. Something, an extremely strong feeling I could not understand, made it impossible to join in. If the situation was 'formal', or organized, part of what was planned, I had no problem. Spontaneous behaviour was a different thing. I was one of the college soloists, even singing in front of hundreds of people was not a problem, and yet I could not do this. It deeply troubled me, and still does.

On the other hand there was the slightly strange student who told me that God had told him I was faking singing bass because my speaking voice was not deep. I could have told him I didn't really know what my voice sounded like and wasn't consciously doing anything except trying to hit the right notes. God does speak to people, but I think the people who are most vulnerable to being deceived or misled by such a claim are those who truly believe that such experiences are possible. People's pronouncements that God has spoken to them should never be automatically accepted. St. Paul taught that a prophet's utterances should always be tested. In my case it was easy. I knew he was wrong.

Yet the knowledge that such claims can be false is often depressing. One can despair and conclude that all such assertions are the self-deceiving products of the incredibly complex calculator that is the human mind. One can be tempted to reject everything because so much seems false, so deluded. In fact, there is so much error and destructive behaviour done in the name of religion, so much of the erroneous "swimming along with the genuine", that one can easily be tempted to toss out all in the face of the infuriatingly false and insincere. I would sympathetically suggest that such a radical and tempting intellectual decision might be equally erroneous and equally destructive, if only to oneself.

Early in my first year I happened to be talking to a third year student, Max Hultgren, who began speaking to me about an unusual kind of prayer. The year before, a teacher from the US, Dr. Beutler, had given a series of sermons on waiting on God. It had been a time of great blessing. This student asked me if I wanted to get up early and pray with him. I readily agreed and he told me he would wake me up at five the next morning. This he did, and I promptly went back to sleep. Later that day he came up to me and angrily told me if I wasn't going to get up he wasn't going to waste his time waking me up. I was surprised at his anger and, embarrassed, I asked him to try again. The next morning when he woke me, I got up.

He had explained to me that waiting on God was not prayer in the usual sense of asking God for things, even good things, but silencing one's mind and coming into the presence of God. Telling God you wanted to be in his presence was perhaps the one thought one consciously did. Stopping one's thoughts is not particularly easy. In the silence of the dark prayer room it was only a little easier. Getting up at five became a habit, and continued for some time, though with no apparent change in my spiritual life.

What went on in the prayer room was that I would come to God, silence my mind for some period of time, after a while begin to think about various things, fall asleep and then wake up and attempt once more to be silent before God. It wasn't working, and I, slightly desperately, asked Max how long it would take. Of course he could not answer this question. Then I began to notice changes. Perhaps I was a little more loving. One time in chapel the Holy Spirit came down powerfully upon me and I gave a message in tongues. If all of that sounds alien, or even ridiculous, there is nothing I can do to relieve you, though I ask that you trust me when I say that mentioning it was not so that you would think wonderfully of me.

The truly wonderful thing that did occur was that, though I had never once thought of this when I was waiting on God, I suddenly realized I no longer hated my father. I had long understood that hating someone was exceedingly sinful, just read the first epistle of John. There had not been any intellectual reasoning, attempting to assemble arguments to explain to myself, to convince myself why I should forgive him. I had not even thought about him. However, the hatred was gone and forgiveness entered my heart entirely of its own, with no effort on my part.

The truly terrible thing was that I slowly stopped waiting on God and returned to normal prayer. I think the mistake I made was that I thought I had "arrived", that my spiritual life had been so deeply changed, and perhaps unconsciously I must have thought I no longer needed to wait on God (as unreasonable as that may sound).

Yet I believe that God taught me some important lessons from my short stint of waiting. I had done nothing to justify God's blessing in any way. Most of the time I was in the prayer room I was either sleeping or thinking. Yet God came to me. After years of thinking I understood the grace of God I actually did begin to understand that God does bless us, do things for us entirely based on his love and not at all on the basis of the good things we have done, indeed sometimes despite the not so good things we do. That grace really is the undeserved expression of the love of God, that it is not simply a religious word but is active. And I understood this because that was exactly how God had treated me.

I also learned that holiness is written on our hearts by God through the Lord Jesus, such that holiness is put into us so that, rather than being the result of repeated moments of determination to act righteously, righteousness becomes our true nature, taking over more and more of our hearts and character such that we naturally act, as God would act. Indeed, much, though definitely not all, of what is decent behaviour is our valiant struggle not to act as our sinful nature would have us act.

Yet, to achieve this we seem to need to spend time alone with God, silently, giving God time to work in our hearts by the Holy Spirit who lives within us as we live in him. The Lord Jesus is not external to us. Rather he is in us and we are united with him, as Paul in Ephesians and Galatians teaches. It is his presence in us that can produce the holiness we all search for.

Lastly, I found that God heals, and wants to heal our hearts on the psychological level. What God had done for me without my asking, was remove the pain caused by my father's "unintentional" cruelty. I do not think this happens very often, but I believe that is because we do not let God take the time to heal us. Yet, that is what is possible. Though God can heal everyone on the psychological and physical levels, we habitually go to doctors. Nevertheless, God does not, I believe, regard the medical profession as enemies but as co-workers.

I believe that God understands that we are so far from a true knowledge of him that most of the time we will never be in the position to experience physical or psychological divine healing on a universal scale. It would be difficult to determine which of these two areas is more important. I suppose to one who is suffering, the problem one has is the crucial point. I think I speak the truth on this issue. I could not imagine a god of love not wanting suffering to decrease, merely because an individual is not spiritual enough to receive healing only from God, and most of us are not so spiritual.

Over a year the college would receive a number of requests for volunteers to work in various organizations. One of these was for visitors to the local insane asylum at Goodna. This did not sound too appealing to me. Actually, I found it rather frightening. Later, I was praying that God would increase my love for people when, the words "Then go to Goodna" were spoken to me. This "sentence" broke in on my consciousness as if someone external to me, someone I could not see, was speaking to me; it was not felt as a thought I had generated, nor was it the kind of thing I expected. I went, but I think the real meaning of the direction was that if I wanted to learn to love people I had to enter into a world where people were suffering. I do not think I have done this to a truly satisfactory degree.

Such an experience happened once more to me while I was in college, and has not occurred since. The second time, I was kneeling beside my bed praying about general things when two songs, one after the other, began to be sung to me, that is in my consciousness, not by someone near me. The first song was "What He's done for others He'll do for you" and the next was "It's always darkest before the dawning". The first I understood to mean that God would provide a wife for me at some stage in my life. I am sorry but I cannot remember why I thought that was the meaning. The second I did not understand, and am still not sure, though I suspect it relates to my life now. At least I sincerely hope it does.

I did not hear these voices. They were entirely "internal". Whether that makes me less or more insane to some I do not care to judge. I have never felt they were symptoms of insanity and I have never felt the need, for example, to don armour and rush out to battle. On the other hand, while they could have been psychological constructs, a belief in God suggests that God can and does speak to people. Indeed, the great stories of the bible, beginning with the theophany to Hagar, Abraham's slave girl, are stories of God directly communicating with people. To me these internal communications have always carried a level of reality, a sense of qualitative difference that tells me that God was speaking to me, as insignificant as I am in the vast cosmic story.

On Saturday and Sunday nights some of the students would catch the train downtown to speak to the people walking along the sidewalk or, with a group, give extempore little "sermons" from the side of the road to passers-by as they walked along. It was not uncommon for small crowds of people to stop for a moment to listen to what we were telling them. I sometimes found myself with this little group of preachers and did not hesitate to stand and tell people of their need and path to salvation. The freedom, and even ability with which I spoke, at this late stage in my life, amazes me, and I am certain that I could not now do this.

It was a different time, and apart from the other students and myself there was an organization, The Open Air Campaigners who did similar things. And unless I am dreaming this, I believe we sometimes had a piano accordion and would stop preaching to sing simple hymns and choruses. In fact, the Salvation Army on Sunday nights would march down the street with their band on their way to the Sally Ann meeting place. Society had a more religious sense at this time and I do not think we, or the Salvation Army, offended too many people, even "self-aware" sinners.

Not everything in college was deeply spiritual. Though we called each other brother or sister, some looked on particular brothers or sisters with a more romantic than fraternal or sisterly affection. Less consuming friendships were also formed that would continue into the future even as some romantic connections would struggle to be so lasting. No one I was acquainted with at college was free of the often sad vicissitudes of human life, simply because we were all there to increase our devotion to God.

Elegy
Each day in chapel
they sang and prayed
and on the streets preached
the good news to the lost,
no duplicity
in their young souls.
They were my friends

> *sisters and brothers*
> *unaware of the great rift*
> *within their hearts*
> *and the disgrace, divorce*
> *and drunken deaths*
> *awaiting them*
> *as surely as each day*
> *our path led us all to chapel*
> *to sing and pray.*

One of the students in my class year was from New Zealand, a biker who before becoming a Christian had been something of a troublemaker. He became my friend. Later, when I was a student at teacher's college in Canada I would befriend and be befriended by a girl to such a degree that we went everywhere together. No doubt most of the other students saw us as girl-friend and boyfriend. This, however, was not the basis or motivation of our friendship. In fact, even now I am unsure what caused such a powerful bond to develop between us. Such was the strength of the friendship between this boy and myself.

I also believe that the strength and expression of this friend-ship was the cause of its destruction. When I would come back to the college in the afternoon after working to earn money to pay the school fees I would always ask if my friend was in the college. I imagine I must have spent a lot of time with him as well, and this can only have been noticed by the other students. I do not think this kind of friendship is common. I did not write the word "normal". I can only think that others must have made jokes about this to my friend, and that, in the end, this caused him to feel embarrassment at the relationship. If one has not experienced such a friendship between another of the same gender, it is not surprising that viewing such a relationship can only seem homosexual. Yet the truth of the matter is that we were both decidedly heterosexual.

He began to make fun of me, to the extent that I felt the only way I could protect myself from him was to completely refuse to speak to him. I could not see any other way of dealing with this. I am not sure of the chronology of what I am about to relate but I believe it occurred after I cut myself off from him.

There was a very pretty, sensual girl in the college and one night he and this girl went a short distance away from the college buildings into a grassy area. I suspect he was going to try to make love to her, but in the course of this, something happened that quite terrified him. Though I remember what he told me, I am not sure what this was, or even if he was justified in being afraid. That is, however, irrelevant. He came to my room where there were three other students sleeping and in great fear wanted to get into bed with me. This he did, just lying there. I do not remember how long that went on but there was no suggestion of sexual activity on either his part or mine.

I do not remember that we had a close friendship of any kind after that and he did not come back the next year because he had had a physical relationship with a girl at a summer camp in New Zealand that resulted in his absence from college in my second year.

I understand that the relationship between King David and Jonathon, the son of King Saul is often seen, though usually not spoken of, as a homosexual or bi-sexual relationship. It may have been, but from my experience it may well not have been. The run of the mill understanding of human relationships is very simple. Complications and unusual relationships are not part of the usual calculation. My fellow students were quite probably more kind than most would have been in the situation. Nevertheless, if *they were* the cause, they got our friendship wrong and effectively ended it.

I do not feel animosity towards them. I have never been conscious of such a feeling. The only feeling I have is amazement at the depth of the friendship I felt for this person, amazement and an unanswered wonder that it ever happened.

The college had a rule that after lights out the students were not permitted to leave the college grounds. Not far from the college lived a middle aged Christian woman, a Mrs. Corrigan, and her husband. Quite often my friend and I would leave the college and walk to their house to spend time with them. They were excellent Christians and we would talk, probably have a cup of tea with them and have good fellowship with them before we went off into the darkness back to the college. In reflection, I never considered if the rule was good or bad. It was just unimportant, and the intent in going temporarily AWOL was not pleasure but human and Christian fellowship. I wonder, though, why I have never felt guilty about this.

I have, however, long felt great guilt about what I did to hurt one of the girls in second or third year. I was very much aware that I did not have a girlfriend, and though I did not feel particularly attracted to this girl I communicated the idea to her that I felt romantically inclined towards her. As it happened, Dr. Beutler returned to our college to give a series of teaching sermons.

Exactly at this time I was told that the girl I was misleading, though I would never have said this at the time, returned my "affections". During one of this man's sermons God told me that I definitely must not have a relationship with her. This was not communicated in a series of words but rather in a very strong feeling that contained this idea. Only I know if God actually told me this, but knowing that we can psychologically deceive ourselves, this possibility also exists. I, however, believe that God did tell me not to do this, and given my emotional dishonesty with the girl, it was almost certainly the correct thing to do. I am sure I hurt this perfectly nice person to some degree and I have felt guilt and perhaps shame for all the years since.

After Bible college my brother in law, who had been a third year student when I was in first year, asked me to come down to Adelaide and help him with a Slavic church he was pastoring. In college, during my first year, he had been one of the four students in my room. Often, on Sundays I would ride on the back of his motorcycle when he visited Slavic Christians before their Sunday service. His stories about God's protection and guidance in China, where he was born, were fascinating and amazing and strengthened my faith in the reality of God. Anyway, in Adelaide it was agreed that I would preach every Sunday evening in English and he would look after the Russian side. This went well for a period only to be stopped by the older Slavic members who were concerned that the young people were losing their Slavic heritage and forgetting their parents' language.

At that point I got a job in a steel factory, the British Tube Mills that now made gas cylinders, though during the war they had made bombs. The factory operated 24 hours a day and so the workers, including myself, cycled through these eight-hour shifts. One of the workers, in a section where I would put steel chains around a number of long steel tubes and lower them into a huge acid bath to remove any rust, a young guy, used to make fun of me because of my Christianity yet something, perhaps because I did not respond with abuse to his repeated taunts, changed his attitude and we became good friends. Surprisingly, he even came to my defense when others attempted to make fun of me. How wonderful.

Following this I worked in a hospital in the sterilizing unit. This was a very happy time and the workers were always singing. It was a surprisingly friendly place to work. I remember one of the older ladies always calling me "love". She must have been British.

I had also found a dynamic church in the Klemzig Assemblies of God and began to make friends there, not doing anything much except occasionally singing duets with the wife of one of the people with whom I had become friends and at whose house I spent many pleasant Sunday afternoons. I saw this man almost in a fatherly light, though in retrospect he cannot have been much older than I was. He seemed in control of his life and untroubled by any doubt, while I felt somehow like a child. This is odd, as even when I was a teenager and later when I was in Bible College, I do not think I ever felt like this. In fact, for the short time I was preaching every Sunday night for my brother-in-law, I also did not feel this way.

In stark contrast to today's usual weekly agenda the church had a bible study and prayer meeting on Wednesdays, a youth meeting on Saturday night, which was not a "games night" and two services on Sunday, the morning service a worship service and the evening one always a gospel service, and this rather full program was loyally attended by most of the congregation. Surprisingly, even on a Sunday there was time for other pastimes. On Saturday nights, after the youth meeting, I would sometimes drive up into the Mt. Lofty range and park my car beside the road with the city lights sparkling on the plain below, the roads, straight lines in all directions. The seats in the car were very comfortable and I would sleep until early morning and then drive "home".

> *Memories of a Girl.*
> *Was it the car*
> *I slept in*
> *by the side of the road*
> *in the Adelaide hills*
> *on Saturday nights,*
> *so I could drive down the*
> *empty winding road*
> *at sunrise*
> *to the still sleeping city*
> *on the plain below,*
> *or the fear filled love*
> *I felt for Perry Tippet*
> *as she sat beside me*
> *on the way to Victor Harbour ?*
> *For all I know*

the car may still survive.
How insignificant
those feelings seem
looking back
at these old photos.

I was aware of caring romantically for this girl in the poem who was also a member of the church I was attending but as I would later come to understand, it never occurred to me to do anything romantic with her. It never even entered my head to try to hold her hand, let alone anything more physically romantic. I can now theorize why, psychologically that was so, but I am still amazed at how radically absent all such thoughts were from my consciousness. Ignoring the fact that she had never completely forgotten a boyfriend she had fairly recently broken up with.

Last night
I bought the blues record
she liked,
the girl from Victor Harbour
who could
never quite forget
someone else.

Some time after my brother in law finished pastoring the Slavic church, he began a drug addict and criminal rehabilitation centre. This had begun with the referral of a drug addict by the court to his centre. As time went on, other troubled people, such as prostitutes and alcoholics came to live in the large house he and my sister had taken. I also lived there with them, but I was not actively involved in the running of the centre.

Australia at this time had very few gunmen but one of these, a friend of a prostitute who had been converted, came one night and visited us, sitting at our table and having a lovely unthreatening conversation with all of us. The husband of the converted prostitute was a safe cracker, and she and I, for some forgotten reason, were in a car with him when in the middle of an argument they were having she grabbed the gearshift and tried to tear it off the steering column. Things became a little dangerous at this point and we both jumped out of the car and tried to escape into an unknown neighbour's house telling the neighbour in very broken Portuguese that we were in danger of being killed. Obviously this did not occur.

Margo

*It was her terrible
unhappiness
that made him ask her
to church.
She had a record
as they say
as long as your arm
and he a short memory,
a necessary quality
for a married man
with a prostitute.
She was not beautiful
but she knew the crims
and how to turn a trick
just not how to escape
herself.
I met her
after he and his wife
had taken her
to church and God.
I don't blame God
or her
but sometimes it's simply*

not enough.
One day
I was told years later
she put her head into
an oven
and turned on the gas.
Nothing in the world
could touch her
after that..

My brother in law was part of a Russian Pentecostal community that had escaped from Siberia and travelled to China, to Urumchi, a city in a North Western province of China where he was born. When they had to escape from China after the communist revolution there, the community had divided into two groups, one going to South America, Uruguay I believe, and the other sailing to Australia. However, they all believed they would eventually end up in a city called London in Canada that none of them had ever been to. My brother in law and my sister, as a result of this belief, ultimately migrated to Canada in 1968, and after they invited me to follow them, I moved there as well, a year later, though not for the same reason.

I have often told people that migrating to Canada was like crossing the street. There was no great emotion involved. I applied, was accepted, got on a plane and eventually arrived in the South Western Ontario city I was to spend several years in.

While I was blithely discovering a new country I did not think about the impact my leaving would have on my family in Australia, or the almost certain suffering it would cause in my mother as I carelessly travelled off and left them behind. The thought that her child, her eldest son could leave and choose to live thousands of miles away, as if his mother did not matter could well have been devastating.

I do not know how my father reacted. My first thought is that he would not have particularly cared, but I do not have the right to think this. In fact, I much later discovered that he had a quite sympathetic view of my sister's and my move fifteen odd thousand miles from them.

There is, however, some truth in this indifference of mine. I did not feel any need or desire to be near them, did not feel any deep closeness that would have caused some hesitation in my plans. I do not know if my brothers and sister felt my sister and I were thoughtlessly abandoning them, that we did not care for them. They may well have felt this, but almost certainly this would have been how my mother, and possibly even my father, actually felt.

In my old age I have come to understand this unintended thoughtlessness on my part. It was not that I wanted to get far away from my family. Nor did it enter my mind that I might be causing terrible unhappiness to them. I come very close to believing that they were simply not important to me, and the realization leaves me speechless. As I put myself in their hearts I find it almost impossible to face the pain I most probably caused.

My first job in London was cleaning offices at night, but the second job was far more interesting, though also done mostly at night. This was driving taxi in a city I had just arrived in, and which I was completely unfamiliar with. I usually worked a twelve hour shift, and my first bit of cultural education came when the radio dispatcher told me to stop calling him "mate", a common way of addressing someone, usually male, in Australia. Just as well I didn't call him "cobber", meaning the same thing. Who knows what he would have said at that!

In the course of my life as a taxi driver I was forced to change a tire in the middle of a snowstorm, and clean pools of blood from the back seat of the car after picking someone up from one of the London hospitals. I also found myself threatened in the middle of the night by a moderately drunk First Nations passenger, for which the local police followed me out of the city to the reservation to make sure I remained unharmed and for which, even now, I am extremely grateful. Nevertheless, the most interesting event was driving a motorcycle gang member to an unlicensed house that sold after hours alcohol, and being given his "business" card. I drove the cab. What someone did after they got out of the cab was not, I believe, my responsibility and anyway, I was not about to tell him that what he was doing was illegal. He was a big guy, whose name was Tiny, and he was actually quite friendly. After the second time he told me to call him if I ever needed any "help". I thanked him.

I continued this job while I was going to Teacher's College, and after one of the local drivers was murdered I also made a point of praying for protection every time I drove. It didn't pay well, but I suppose it kept me alive.

Canada?

I was living in Adelaide before I left for Canada from Brisbane, where my parents and family lived. I had a Morris 1100 and the distance between Adelaide and Brisbane, choosing the route I wanted to take, was about 1500 miles. I had driven about 7 or 800 miles when the gear system began to give me trouble. I could not keep the car in third gear at all. In fact, I could not even keep the car in second gear without wrapping my leg around the gear shift, which fortunately was on the floor of the car, and keeping it there for the entire time.

I cannot remember if I stopped off at a garage in Armidale, where my uncle used to live, or Tamworth, where my sister used to live. At any rate, I attempted to see neither of them. I had almost no money and my only goal was to get home to Brisbane. I was told I could not drive at more than 45 or 50 in second gear if I didn't want to burn out the gear system, and even that was too high. So I drove home for the last 300 odd miles with my leg wrapped around the gear stick, almost certainly damaging the gear system because I certainly drove at those speeds. When I finally took off for Canada, I left the car with my parents to get rid of. I do not remember if I had completely paid for the car. Nor do I remember any arrangements I had made with my parents for the sale of the car. Indeed, I do not think I made any arrangements. Like a ten year old child, I think I simply left all this for them.

I am not sure if the jet I left Australia on was a 707 or a 747, though at that time it must have been a 707. The first stop was in Fiji at Nandi, the main airport. I had to wait several hours before the next flight to Honolulu and so asked an Indian taxi driver to drive me around so I could see some of the country. Talking to the driver was interesting and he asked if I would like to rest at his family's house until I needed to catch the plane. After meeting his family I went into one of the rooms and fell asleep. He had arranged to wake me up when it was time to go.

Two things amaze me about this at this late stage of my life. I obviously completely trusted this complete stranger. 'Trust and stranger' do not seem to go together, yet I felt no sense of danger. Secondly, though I was extremely grateful to him and his family I gave them nothing to express this and I wonder if they expected something. I think I have always thought gratitude was a sufficient "return" for someone's kindness, but perhaps I am wrong. The taxi driver's family were not wealthy.

Hawaii was really my introduction to North American life. The stretch limos at the airport, the Arizona memorial, the vast military cemetery in the crater of an extinct volcano, police wearing guns, and milkshakes that were more money than I wanted to pay, were all new and fascinating. Also, the day after the Fourth of July, I could not have arrived at a more patriotic time. I was truly impressed. I have learned since that the first moon landing also happened at this time, but I knew nothing about it. How can I have been so completely ignorant of such a historic event, yet such is the case.

I landed in the continental USA in Los Angeles where, I think I was met by the family of one of the students of the Wycliffe Bible Translators linguistics course we had both done in Brisbane at Cromwell College on the campus of the University of Queensland. We all went to church together but they also took me to Disneyland, which is a slightly different kind of "church". From L.A. I flew to San Francisco where I stayed for a few days with relatives of my sister's husband, and from there I took a Greyhound across the country to Canada. Utah was incredibly hot and apparently, while I was asleep I kicked open one of the windows of the extremely hot bus. The journey across the continent finally did come to an end and on the 27th of July, 1969 I was given landed immigrant ID and entered Canada.

One of the first things I felt I had to do, apart from getting a job, was apply to teacher's college. Sometime, probably in my first year at Bible College I began to study four high school subjects so that I could finish high school. I'm not certain how many subjects I needed to do this but I got passing grades in three of these and something that was not a grade but also not a failure with the other. Somehow, these courses and perhaps my time in Bible College were enough for me to gain entrance to London Teacher's College, less than impressive though this was.

I have never been a disciplined student, though this does not fill me with any sense of pride. I have gone through an academic life based, I suspect, on emotion. If I was truly interested in a subject I would put a lot of energy into it, and usually did well. If, however, the subject was simply something I had to do, I would deal with it in quite a desultory fashion, putting into it only that level of interest and energy that would allow me to pass the subject.

Whether this reveals a character defect on my part, or is the result of never being encouraged by parents to work hard on schoolwork in order to achieve good grades I am not sure. Indeed, there may possibly be other reasons I have not thought of.

The fact remains, though, that for most of my academic life I have depended almost exclusively on my native intelligence to achieve my goals, which have, themselves, almost certainly been only half heartedly sought after, though that I suspect is because there was nothing clear, linking the study program to an end goal.

The unfortunate truth is that I do not believe I have ever had long-term goals that gave any genuine direction to my studies. I did not go to Bible College with any thought out plan to enter any specific ministry. Though almost every other student had already arranged with multitudinous school boards to arrange where they were going to teach, I did not attend Teacher's College with any idea of teaching in any specific school district. My undergraduate program did not have any particular goal in mind and I never contacted any organization to make use of the knowledge or skills I had attained there. My attendance at two seminaries likewise was focussed on nothing more than the degrees themselves, and graduate school was simply and mainly motivated by the final attaining of the degree.

It was not that I did not want to work and therefore continued studying. I worked every year I was in post secondary education, at times in separate jobs in different institutions. The odd thing is that if one were to look at my history of study and employment, I could easily be thought of as an extremely hard working individual. I drove taxis twelve hours a day while I was at Teacher's College and in Australia, while I was in seminary, taught at two colleges each week, while at the same time doing courses on a completely different degree at the University of Queensland. This rather directionless characteristic is, however, one of the most dominant aspects of my personality.

Teacher's College was my introduction to Canadian life and culture, mediated through the eyes and conversations of my fellow students. One of these students, a girl named Gabrielle took me under her wing without any such words being mentioned and became a friend with whom I spent almost all the time I was in college and many, many hours after classes, shopping and travelling around the city. Probably the other students thought we had a romantic relationship but it was entirely Platonic. She was engaged at the time and I do not think her boyfriend was ever troubled about our relationship, though on the other hand I do not remember that I ever met him until the very end of the course when our ways parted.

Strangely, I seemed to attend a number of weddings while I was a student at LTC. This caused me a great deal of unhappiness. I could not dance, and the more I went to these celebrations the more depressed I became. The solution came suddenly and from an unexpected source. A girl in my class, one I had never really thought about or even spoken to, came over to where I was standing sadly, and simply led me onto the dance floor. What she and I said and did I cannot recall, and on top of that I didn't have a clue about how to dance, but from that moment I had no problem. As far as I am concerned, she could have been an angel, for I have no idea who she was. How grateful I am to that unremembered girl.

At this time, another student and I rented rooms in a house about a mile or so from the college beside a CNR railway track, and I became so used to hearing the trains pass that I soon ceased to hear them at all. The little house on Beaconsfield Street was just off the road that led to both the university and Teacher's College, and to catch a bus home from school I had to walk up to the university where the buses would stop to let off and pick up the university students.

Once, during a snowstorm, I remember walking the short distance up from the college to the bus stop in the university with the snow blowing fiercely, almost straight at me. Angrily, I said, "You're trying to get me, aren't you!" obviously believing in the sentient nature of all existence when it became a personal obstacle to my progress.

I had long thought of university as a locus of pride, if not in the people who were associated with it then, potentially in me if I were to become such a one. Evangelicals as a group are deeply suspicious of universities as places where religious and biblical theories contrary to orthodox belief are generated and where the faith of believers is weakened and too frequently lost. Indeed, in the Religious Studies Department at the University of Queensland, I was told that out of the entire faculty, only one professor believed in God.

I discovered that the husband of one of my fellow students at Teacher's College was doing a PhD in English at the university. I visited their apartment in Campus housing and found both of them to be a friendly unassuming couple. Often I had to wait for a bus in the afternoon and to kill time I would go to the university cafeteria. There I watched people and listened to them and found them to be completely normal and unpretentious. I thought to myself that they were no different to me and came to the conclusion that I could also do what they were doing. I realize, of course, that this conclusion was based on rather shallow "research", but I decided to apply to the university for the coming Fall semester and was accepted.

I began an Arts degree program the following September and slowly discovered that university work was qualitatively different to anything I had done in high school, or even Teacher's College. An English professor, with the unlikely name of Tom Collins, patiently showed me, after I told him I didn't see (or even believe) what he had been telling us about a poem he had been teaching us, that there was more in the poem than the surface reading. It took time to acclimatize myself to university practice, but after a couple of years of study I began to be able to use the knowledge I had been rapidly accumulating to analyse and critique assignment questions in a moderately successful manner.

One of my majors was anthropology, and my Linguistics professor, a rather odd young woman from California, invited her students to her apartment for a party. Poking through her books I discovered a Japanese novel that looked interesting and asked if I could borrow it. This began a love affair with all things Japanese, but especially literature and history, that is now reflected in my own book collection.

Apart from certain courses I enjoyed I was able to make new friends with several of the students, not all in my year, and not all in Arts, who were very intelligent and broadened my vision of the world of ideas. I also found that there were Evangelical students and others who were not Christians at all, who were not particularly insane, some of whom became lifelong friends. I think I love this first degree more than any other degree I have attained. Occasionally I would skip classes, but usually my friends and I would meet in a cafeteria and discuss some interesting idea, philosophy, or politics, so even while skipping a class, I never felt I was wasting my time.

At the risk of sounding unsophisticated, learning at this time was an exciting experience of discovery. As I wrote essays... ideas, theories, possibilities seemed to flow out of the tip of my pen. Ideas I had not thought of suddenly appeared before me as the essay I was writing (at times almost illegibly) on large sheets of waste computer paper, took shape. It was not that I did no research or that my desk was not covered with books that I had read on the subject. Learning was such a pleasure. This experience of discovery so affected me that I forever became an opponent of the structured, pre-thought out essay model that is taught in many, if not most schools, where the conclusion is already decided on, and where nothing is discovered, the writing process is totally mechanical, the paragraphs micro-structured and the entire experience ultimately boring.

There are those who say the "hippie" movement died out at the end of the 60's. This is not the case. It may have died out after the mid-seventies but when I was at Western it was alive and well. There are evangelicals who look down on the hippie movement, but there were important values that were part of its unusual ability to attract young people, especially its anti-materialistic position and its emphasis on love and peace. That there were aspects that were not positive may merely say something about all social and religious movements. Nothing human comes, and definitely does not end up, perfectly "clean". Jesus freaks, who were the Christian form of hippies, were young people who identified with the positive values of the movement and sought to express their Christian faith in ways and clothing that reflected this new, and ultimately doomed rejection of a materialist social philosophy.

Few students were unaffected by the spirit of this movement and neither was I. I wore a silver coloured tear shaped peace symbol around my neck and like most other students, met other young people with the two fingered V of my left hand and the word "peace". This must sound embarrassingly naïve and immature at this cynical time but we innocently meant it. I also had a woven leather bracelet on my left wrist and wore white jeans, various kinds of Indian shirts and Indian sandals. It was comfortable and liberating clothing. Obviously, I was assimilating and being socialized into the dominant youth culture.

For two or three summer holidays, while at university, I drove around Canada. From a university friend who lived about thirty miles north of London I was able to get a job driving Winnebago RVs from the factory in his little town to dealerships all over the country. This friend, who was at the end of his second year in Law school, was offered, and took a job, strange as it may now sound, as a judge in Newfoundland. I never heard from him again, but I hope his life was as happy and serendipitous as the odd job offer.

I drove these vans to varying places, from Vancouver to the East coast, and North to Timmins, sleeping in the vans until I got to the required location, after which I would take a bus or train back to London. The fact that I was able to take a train from Vancouver to London without spending more than I had actually just earned says, I suspect, something about both money and the general price of things before OPEC decided to shake up the world economy. I wasn't paid very much for the privilege; I think it was about 17 cents a mile, but it kept me alive during the summer, after which I would get my job back in the university library to pay for the rest of the year.

I was never conscious of it but moving to this new country was deeply psychologically disrupting, not in the sense of creating a psychological problem, but more in the way of forcing me to create, to learn a new inner map of my surroundings, the local and national institutions, and the ways people thought and felt in this country. I no longer had social entities I knew intimately and could evaluate, and no places or organizations I had, in Australia, habitually associated with and derived comfort from.

Not only was the country new and unknown, my new friends belonged to different churches, even though they were dedicated Christians. As a consequence, rather than going to a Pentecostal church, I began attending an Anglican church led by an Evangelical returned missionary from India. Parenthetically, he and his wife had five daughters, two of whom married two of my friends while I almost married another.

Becoming a Canadian was one of the simplest things I have ever done. My friend and I were walking downtown in London (Ontario) and near the main Post Office where the citizenship office was located, we decided to apply for citizenship. As I recall the whole thing was unpremeditated. We both went up to the office and told them we wanted to become Canadians. No problem. As he was from Britain and I was a member of the British Commonwealth, we were informed this could be done quite simply. I paid the lady $10, raised my arm and swore allegiance to the Queen (and possibly Canada) and with that done it was simply a matter of waiting for the paperwork.

Oh, how simple (and inexpensive) life was back in the good ole days. It was a time when students could afford to buy their required books…and kept them, where even if you were a student you could travel in the summer, as I did myself, where the school fees were not so onerous that you would be paying for them for years after you graduated. Inflation does not provide a satisfactory reason for why things are different these days. Greed, on the other hand, might be an answer.

If I could, in this vein, a small comment on the ten dollars. It is common these days to hear commentators say, "oh, but that was a lot of money back then." This, however, is both correct and incorrect. Compared to ten dollars now it was certainly worth more than ten dollars is now, but on the other hand, ten dollars back then was not thought to be a lot of money. Within a year of arriving in Canada, working part time and going to college I bought a three or four year old 1966 Mustang for $1200. Today, comparatively speaking, this would have been next to impossible. I was a student working at, at least one part time job to pay for food, rent, and everything else, and yet paying the ten dollars did not inconvenience me at all. Incidentally, the price of gas at this time was 32 cents a gallon, which is about 8 cents a litre. The truth is, even when the variable of inflation is included, most things in the early seventies were not expensive. That reality would come later.

After I completed the Arts degree at Western I applied to a Low Church seminary in Toronto that was part of the University of Toronto. The college was an old, not very attractive brick building about one block long immediately in front of the much more beautiful Hart House where I eventually read Dostoyevsky novels in its tiny downstairs coffee shop. Directly across the street from the seminary I was attending was another much more glorious Gothic building, Trinity College where students with a more Anglo-Catholic bent did their theological training. It was not that we did all our theology in the college where we resided. Courses towards the M.Div. we were studying for could be done at any number of denominational colleges, and in the two years I was a student here I took courses in Trinity, the United Church college and a Catholic seminary, as well as the college I was a resident in.

During the second semester of my second year at Wycliffe I registered to do two reading courses with a Catholic theologian named Dr. Gibson. I chose to do one on Kierkegaard and the other on Nietzsche. Both of these writers interested me deeply. Kierkegaard was a wonderful extremist who passionately wanted Christians to experience God and free themselves from an ossified religious faith. Nietzsche was an atheist who would have wanted to be a Christian if the church had ever been able to express any real faith and behaviour. I 'loved' both of them.

In Bible College I had been shown an interesting structure that could be used to reveal the internal shape of all of the books of the bible. For some reason, I attempted to dissect one of Nietzsche's books in this manner. It seemed to work, and I was able to reveal a Chiastic structure (that is a structure in the shape of the Greek letter Chi, the first letter of the Greek word Christos/Christ) to Nietzsche's book. My teacher wrote that the work was brilliant and original. This no doubt pleased me, but as most of the other courses I was registered in were not so particularly brilliant it never occurred to me to change the way I thought about myself. I suppose it is like being told one time that one is beautiful and never hearing such wonderful praise ever again.

Over the intervening years I have thought about this paper and I seriously doubt that Nietzsche ever intended his book to be viewed in this way or indeed that he had written it with this structure in mind. Yet, if I am right in this, how was it possible to fit the book into what was the fairly complex structure that I used? Further, does this not put into question other "findings" that are the result of data fitting other complex structures?

I paid my fees and earned living expenses working at two part time jobs. One was in the college and the other was in the Robarts U of T library. This was just up the street from the college and mainly involved shelving books, as I had done at Western. Probably in second year I was the night watchman of Wycliffe College. I would walk around the college to make sure all was well, and at a certain time, can't remember when, I would lock all the doors. Theoretically everyone was supposed to be inside by this time but there were usually stragglers. As the night wore on and I would get progressively sleepier I would go into the large room beside the entrance, lie down on a couch and sleep. I wasn't really supposed to do this and it could have been dangerous for the college. but I didn't expect anything to happen and when a really late student would bang on the door I would get up, let them in and go back to the couch. I think I was extremely fortunate that nothing ever did happen.

At the time I was a student here, one no longer had to wear classical gowns to class and meals but there remained a rule that one had to wear a jacket to enter the dining hall. I did not have one, nor did I have the money to buy one. This troubled and embarrassed me and I spoke to one of my professors, Jacob Jocz a Jewish Christian priest from Lithuania, one of the Baltic states, who had a reputation for being understanding as well as intelligent. I have no idea where he got it but he gave me a jacket. Naturally, I was deeply thankful.

I would be failing to express gratitude, on another level, if I did not mention two students who became close friends. One, rather than being Anglican was a member of the Christian Missionary Alliance named Glen Shellrude. He had gotten his BA from the American University in Beirut and later went on to get a doctorate in theology after which he taught in the Philippines. The other, named Richard Tanner became a Canon in the Anglican Church. Richard was a remarkable person whose courage and loyalty to me I will never forget, and is known to God. I lost contact with him for many years and serendipitously met him at a conference I was attending at Lake Louise where he was one of the speakers.

It was while I was in seminary here that I fell in love with the eldest daughter of the returned missionary in London. It was an interesting relationship in which there was no physical contact. At the time this lack never entered my head and it was not as if, in some magnificent struggle to remain pure, I was restraining myself. Yet, there have been very few people with whom I have ever shared ideas and myself as I did with her. I imagine this lack of physicality in the relationship must appear odd to most people. Indeed, looking back I know it was unusual. It must also have been rather unsatisfying from her side. Perhaps some degree of explanation will appear later.

At the end of my first academic year in seminary I applied to teach for the summer in Australia and was assigned to a high school on the Gold Coast near where my mother was living. In the course of the summer break I found I had lost interest in the girl I had been in love with, and just mentioned. When I returned I discovered that this very fascinating person whom I had been courting, and whom I now was no longer interested in, was now "in love" with me. Once again, particularly bad timing, you will agree.

I continued to see her over my second year at seminary and was eventually strongly advised to ask her to marry me. I believe I made a completely unromantic proposal in obedience to this advice, the result of which was totally predictable. Another man who was in the acting group she was in was actually in love with her and I agreed that going with him was better than wasting her time with me. We parted friends and I hope we still are. On my part, this was a typically ridiculous romance.

By the end of my second year at seminary I came to believe I could not become an Anglican priest, or indeed, any kind of minister. It was not that I had lost my faith, but perhaps I had questions that I felt would have made it difficult to preach with any degree of confidence and assurance. The courses I was taking did not contribute to this dilemma. None of the courses I have taken has ever had such a result. If anything, it was simply suffering, though not necessarily my own, that left me so unsure. I decided to leave seminary, and for want of any better idea, return to Western and do a year of philosophy. As it turned out, this did not resolve any of the questions I had in relation to God, but neither did it make the struggle any worse.

Nor was it merely the theoretical problem of suffering that troubled me so much. The problem was that believing, as I did, in the omniscience of God, how could God, knowing what would occur from the first moment of creation, create a universe in which there was an almost equal amount of destruction and death (in a broad understanding of that word) as there was beauty and wholeness? And moreover, given that there are approximately seven billion people on the planet, most of whom have no idea about the path of salvation through Christ, and that this, if not the number, has been the case from the beginning of Christianity, and which must necessarily include the millions living in what is traditionally understood as Christian countries, how could this God send most to an eternal hell, for in all orthodox Christian teaching is this not so?

> *Don't tell me life's*
> *a gift*
> *a gift can be refused*
> *and who's been given such*
> *a choice?*
> *And if the gift's returned*
> *does that give freedom*
> *and peace?*
> *Van Diemen's, they say*
> *was the cruelest of places*
> *ofttimes for the simplest of crimes*
> *what then hell*
> *we're told is*
> *endless.*
> *Who is this jailer*
> *who makes us eternal*
> *without asking*
> *if we want the gift*

then tells us,
truthfully, for sure,
that we're all sinners?
Perhaps you're willing
to worship a god
who sends
most recipients of the gift of life
to hell.
Blame them.
You're ok.
But then haven't you forgotten,
repentance is also a gift?
Life is a dubious enough gift.
If this is the god you worship
I wonder what you will
discover
when you meet him.
For me,
that nightmare
is too horrible for thought
I choose to dream
a God
with no such lusts.

The unsaved millions have long been the motivation for gospel preaching at home and through the global missionary work of the last 200 odd years, as indeed it should be. However, this global preaching does not solve the problem that the majority of the world's population dies without hearing of Jesus, let alone choosing to either accept or reject him.

So, given the omniscience of God and the tiny number of people who are saved, what, I thought, did this say about the character of God? In addition, if I thanked God for my food did this not imply that those dying of starvation had not been so supplied? Were these more sinful than I and the millions in

the West who have more than enough food and more often than
not did not care at all about God? I could not believe it.

> *It has been said*
> *my love is but a small reflection*
> *of the love God has for me,*
> *but as I watch my child with love*
> *I wonder,*
> *can this be ?*

> *What is it in your word*
> *I should believe ?*
> *You say you love*
> *yet act*
> *as one who does not understand*
> *the tyranny of sin.*
> *If there is nought*
> *that I can do to save myself,*
> *why do you roar,*
> *as if I sin*
> *with great delight ?*
> *Do you not think*
> *you have yourself to blame ?*
> *Why do you hide*
> *as if it all were clear,*
> *conceal yourself*
> *like a virgin*
> *and then complain*
> *we do not know you ?*
> *If I am born in sin*
> *why do you pursue*
> *with such apparent zeal*
> *to cast me into hell,*
> *yet leave me blind,*
> *unknowing and untouched*

by grace
that is my only hope ?
If e'en the turning is a gift
why then consign
the greater part
to hell
so easily ?
You terrified poor Job.
What reasons did you give ?
We know your power.
Is that the only answer
that you have ?
And if the ones in Sodom
could have changed,
why did you not let them ?
Was your lesson more important
than their eternal souls ?
I sometimes wish
that one could rise in judgment
against you !

If you imagine I was troubled by these ideas because I wanted to rebel against God you would be mistaken. I could no more avoid these thoughts and their implications than I could an oncoming train if I was chained to the railway tracks. You see it was the nature of God and its eternal impacts, if one believed traditional evangelical theology, (actually across the board orthodox theology) that was the problem. These thoughts paralysed my confidence in God for many years, and not finding any resolution to the issue, resulted in a mental battlefield, one side of which was filled with angry questions, while the other could not quite accept what appeared irrefutably logical and obvious, namely that God was not to be trusted and was arbitrarily cruel.

The reason I could not make the final decision against God was that that was not how I had experienced (him).

You ask me
to trust you
and voices within,
others
who have never entertained
a doubt in their lives
all nod their heads,
as if there were no questions,
only answers
in which you are the
greatest and simplest.
I even see myself nodding along
with them,
a stranger walking in the shadows
of an almost forgotten
time of faith,
who seeing
still refuses to make that
logical leap.
You remind me of the air pump
in my aquarium
that fitfully pumps out the air
the fish depend on.
I often think I must get
a new one
but then it works again,
and anyway,
where would I get the money ?
You're just like that,
fitfully showing yourself
just enough
so that we know you're there
but not enough
to dispel the doubts.

Now I'll tell you quite honestly. I can't remember when I chose to 'bet' that God could be trusted, or even why I chose this route. I did not have any answers to the huge questions that had paralysed my faith for more than a decade. However, the way I look at it these days is that based on my experiences with God, which reveal mercy and love in the face of great sinfulness (my own), experiences of God intruding into my fear filled heart and suddenly filling me with a deep peace beyond reasoning, and definitely beyond what I expected or deserved, I choose to give God the benefit of the doubt. I no longer have an unquestioning and unquestioned belief, but I am no longer filled with an angry doubt.

If a central tenet of evangelicalism is the centrality and essentiality of Jesus as the unique Saviour, then I hold traditional orthodox evangelical beliefs. I take Paul's remarks in Romans and Galatians on the work of Christ more seriously and more radically than traditional Evangelicals. I take Paul's comments on a future judgement not only for the lost but also for Christians as central to my stance on the work of salvation.

I take the Pauline teaching on salvation and the Mosaic Law seriously. I take this seriously when I read Jeremiah and Isaiah on 'a new covenant', and when I read parts of what is called the Torah, the five books of Moses, especially where it contradicts Pauline teaching and the book of Hebrews, and even more importantly, when I read the words of Jesus commenting on aspects of the Mosaic Law.

Central to my reading of the bible is the love of God, a god who does not act heartlessly and inconsistently in any of (his) actions. I take sin seriously. I take its objective removal seriously, both now in an individual's life and eschatologically. I take repentance seriously and do not seek to cover the problem with mere words. I do not have an answer to all biblical problems, even if some can be clearly rejected. Probably this is just me, but I think salvation and the health of the church are the only two subjects worth taking seriously.

And now something clearly less serious.... and I wouldn't blame you if you found the above a little tiring: Sometime in this year in which I was working part time in the university library, I met someone and fell in love. (Yes, I know, once again) After some time she told me she wanted to stop seeing me because I obviously wasn't interested in her. I hadn't even kissed her, proving, she felt, the truth of her belief. In desperation I told her I didn't know how to kiss. Indeed, the thought of kissing anyone I cared for, never once came to my mind. With very few words she showed me how. I had long felt that I was like a machine that had all the working parts, but had yet to be turned on (no pun intended). No wonder she felt the way she did. Now, at least and last, that part of my consciousness was working.

She was Indian and later went back to India. I completed my year of philosophy and not knowing what else to do with myself, got a job in the university bookstore. I saved as much as I could from this to travel to India and visit her. Near the end I sold as much of my belongings as I could adding to what I had already saved and left.

Flying into Athens I was told we were going to be late for my connecting flight to Pakistan and India but they could hold the plane so that I could catch it. They rushed me off the plane, put me into a vehicle and took me to the plane waiting for me. It never occurred to me that this was unusual, and I am fairly sure it would never happen today, unless I was a VIP.

I arrived in Bombay early in the heat of the morning with no hotel reservation and no experience of India. Coming out of the airport onto the pavement I was immediately surrounded by twenty or more men, each loudly wanting to carry my bags to wherever I wanted. In confusion more than decision I took none of them and went to a taxi telling the driver to take me to a certain hotel. I had a travel book and tried to get a room in more than one hotel but to no avail. In the end I asked the driver to take me to the Church Missionary Society compound where they were kind enough to give me a place to stay for a few days. David Livingstone had planted a tree that still grew in their compound.

Each morning I would awake to the spicy smells of India cooking. I walked around Bombay, went to the beautiful Bombay Taj Mahal hotel by the ocean and later, unsuspectingly attempted to get on a train I discovered was reserved only for women. Sometime in the course of all this I bought a ticket on a train that would take me to New Delhi.

The carriage I was in was constructed with sleeping areas and though the train was not luxurious it was comfortable. Somewhere on the trip to Delhi a police superintendent, or maybe he was an inspector, named Dutta, struck up a conversation with me and asked me to buy him a camera, I believe, when I returned to Canada. I never thought about the possibility that I would have to pay for this, probably because I never took the request seriously.

I had at last learnt to reserve ahead and had arranged to stay at an Anglican monastery in New Delhi for a few days. From there I travelled by bus through Meerut, Haridwar, and Dehra Dun to a dusty little university town named Roorkie where my friend was living. I visited with her for a short time, gave her all the things I had brought with me that she had asked for, and then boarded another bus for Musoorie, a hill station high in the foothills of the Himalayas. I had applied for a job teaching in a missionary school here and though I had not been given the job, wanted to go there anyway. On being given a room in the school I was led off to afternoon tea where, almost seven thousand feet up in the mountains in India I found myself drinking tea and eating chocolate éclairs.

On the way down the mountain, before the bus began its tortuous descent, I noticed that everyone in the bus prayed. The road was narrow, very windy, and only a few feet from certain death if the bus drove too close to the side of the road. I stayed a few more days in Roorkie, once being mistaken for a Muslim because of my beard, and then, once again took the bus back to New Delhi.

We arrived in the middle of the night and along with my bags I got a pedal rickshaw and asked the "driver" to take me to the YMCA. So he set off in the heat of the Indian summer with me and my heavy bags, peddling me, I knew not how far, to an air-conditioned room. In retrospect the man could have killed me in the darkness and in my total ignorance of both where I was and where I was going in the city. Happily, I arrived safely.

While at the YMCA I bought several Indian batiks and joined a group of tourists going to Agra, the home of the Taj Mahal. As part of the tour we were taken to the deserted royal city of Fatehpur Sikri, which I stupidly did not enter, preferring to drink a coke, while leaning against the wall of the deserted city, with an English tourist who had similarly od'd on historic buildings in the middle of the Indian summer. No one knows why it became deserted and I regret not making the effort to see this mysterious place immensely.

Later on the tour, however, in a world where one is rarely overwhelmed, the Taj Mahal left me in awe and speechless. It surely must be one of the most beautiful buildings in the civilized world. I am filled with thankfulness that I had the chance to see this, to be there and to walk around it.

From New Delhi I took a wonderful train to Calcutta where I stayed in an acceptable hotel. From there I visited Mother Theresa's convent. She was not there but I was able to speak to sister Agatha who was very kind to this probably interrupting tourist. While I was in the cafeteria of the hotel, two Indians who had clearly been playing tennis came in and began talking to me. In the course of the conversation one of them offered to take me to Rabindranath Tagore's house the next day. Tagore had won the Nobel Prize for Literature in 1913 and was a well known educator in India and familiar with both Nehru and Gandhi This the man did, first going to his own residence before driving to Tagore's rather large but simple house. I doubt that I would have gone there if he had not invited me. I deeply appreciated his kindness in giving me the opportunity to see this great man's home and fairly simple belongings.

From Calcutta I think I took a train to Bhubaneswar, the capital of Orissa and where my friend had grown up. Here her uncle met me, took me to a place I could stay and drove me around to interesting places in and near the city. It was in Orissa or Tamil Nadu, I honestly can't remember which, that I attempted to enter a Hindu temple. I was refused entrance, but hearing that I was refused entrance a Hindu man who was about to similarly enter said, "Well if he can't enter neither will I." I have always remembered that with great respect for the unknown man. I stayed only a couple of days but remember lying down and sleeping on the platform while waiting for the train. This memory has been with me for many years, and yet I am not certain it ever happened.

From Bhubaneswar I travelled to Madras where I stayed at the Maharani Hotel. It was in Madras that I bought an ivory statue and a black brass floor lamp about four feet high that can be unscrewed into several differently shaped pieces and which I have never used except as a place to hang various items of clothing.

Next I travelled south by bus from Madras intending to stay in a beach resort in the town of Mahabalipuram where I planned to go to the beach right at the resort and relax. Apart from the beach, where Indian men, socialized into a very puritan view of the female body would gaze unsure whether to enjoy or criticize Western women in swimming costumes, Mahabalipuram is famous for its many large stone sculptures, some right on the beach. Ancient Hindu sculptures, often in temples, show naked men and women in a variety of sexual and non-sexual poses that reveal a view of the human body that finds Westerners as ambivalent as they look at these ancient historical works of art and religion as the Indian men who find themselves staring ambivalently at the female swimmers. I had no plan to view the sculptures at all. My uncultured intention was to rest in my little cabin and go to the beach.

Sometime earlier in the trip, probably a week or so, I must have drunk some unsterilized water. India in the summer is very hot and watching ordinary people get off a bus or something and without a thought going up to a pani walla for a cup of water while I could not was difficult. One time I must have yielded to the temptation, for in the middle of the trip to Mahabalipuram I suddenly became violently ill and vomited right in the aisle of the bus as I tried desperately to get to the door. I can remember this incident only with horror and embarrassment.

When I eventually got outside and stopped vomiting I was surrounded by a small group of men who encouraged me to drink coconut milk as this would settle my stomach. Naturally, I appreciated their advice but I have hated the taste of coconut for my entire life. The bus got back on the road with me in violent pain. When we got to our destination, not at the hotel where I planned to stay, the bus stopped to let people out and wait until it was time to drive the small distance to my hotel. I could see the hotel from where we stopped, about three hundred yards away but the bus driver refused to take me there until finally, I gave him some money.

After I booked in I was taken to my little cabin and lay on the bed unable to move, as every movement brought on intense pain. I lay on the bed watching geckos walk along the walls of the cabin, and when I absolutely had to, the sides of the bathroom. I found out that I had amoebic dysentery and for most of the time I was at the resort I could eat virtually nothing. There was a Catholic medical station nearby and each day I would go there to get an injection that was intended to help me recover. I did improve and I remember on the last day at the resort I was able to eat a semi-decent breakfast. Not only did I not see the famous sculptures, not once did I get down to enjoy the beach.

Somehow I was able to return to Madras and from there travel to Kumbakonam in Tamil Nadu, the home of one of my best friends from university. He had arranged for me to stay at his home and "thither" I went. Their house was simple and at the back was a large well from which they got their water. They also had a cow, and I imagine this was their source of milk. He and his family were Brahmans, the highest class in the caste system. Not only was it theoretically impossible for a Brahman to have anything to do with me, I was also still ill which could only have polluted him and his family even more. Fortunately for me they were very educated and progressive and treated me extremely kindly.

Sometime later, and still somewhat ill, I travelled back to Madras, I believe, and indulging myself, stayed at an expensive hotel before flying back to Canada where I received more medical attention from a tropical diseases department in a hospital in Toronto. Though the plane landed in Switzerland, as one had in Holland and Athens before, I cannot claim to have ever been to Europe except in a purely technical sense, though my daughter has been numerous times and has a special love for the continent.

I had been in India six weeks, and though I became extremely sick at the end of my stay I had seen many historic and beautiful sights and been the recipient of much kindness on the part of more than a few individuals to whom I was a complete stranger. Strangely, though I am filled with wonderful memories of India and have always thought of returning, my diary tells me that I felt extremely lonely and would walk up to and speak to complete strangers simply because they spoke English. Indian culture is extremely different to ours and I obviously felt overwhelmed, surrounded, as I was, by multitudes of "foreigners", though "ferengi" means the same thing and is what the Indians called the English. And yet I cannot recall ever feeling afraid.

Soon after I returned to London two significant events rapidly occurred. On the advice of my sister I bought a house not too far from the university. The other was that I was given a job, within walking distance of my house, in St. Joseph's Hospital as an orderly in the urology ward. My activities in this ward cannot be related as I am sure they would be disgusting to some. The ward was, after all, a urology ward and I had to do daily care for the men who were patients in the ward. I found nothing disgusting in this, but that, I suspect, was because all these things simply had to be done. However, I do not doubt that to the majority of outsiders, most of what I did would certainly seem repulsive.

Permit me, in closing this little section, to make, what to some may appear an offensive policy statement. Though male circumcision may seem a pointless and superfluous operation, it is not. For those who have had to clean the penis of anyone, especially an old man, who has not been circumcised and has not cleaned his penis for a period of time, the job is difficult, must be done carefully and is almost certainly painful for the man being cleaned. Dead skin builds up under the uncircumcised skin and attaches itself to the penis. The only people who cry out against circumcision are those who have never had to clean the uncircumcised penis of an already old and probably ill man. A young strong man can look after himself. A sick old man may not be able to. The benefits of the operation are discovered in old age.

Occasionally I would be assigned to the Emerg and to the Psych ward where I met at least two of my friends. I have only respect for these people. We do not choose to suffer mentally and each human mind has its limits. At other times, another orderly and I would be asked to take someone who had died down to the morgue. A steel frame would be placed over the gurney and a sheet would be placed over this so that no one except staff would know what was being transported. If nothing

else, (other than pay) I hope this gave me a little more understanding of the human condition.

As expected, I suppose, I lived in my house and rented out
the vacant rooms to about three university students, mostly
from the Philosophy Department. I don't recall that we ever
did not get along, and most of the time it was fun. Additionally,
they helped pay the mortgage, which carried an interest rate
of seventeen percent. At that time in my life I can only think
I possessed very little wisdom when it came to money. The
house was in a good location; the students were essentially
paying the mortgage, and real estate values would predictably
go up. In fact, they later went up at least 500% and I would
have made a great deal of money if I had kept the house. As it
is, I complained that the value of the house was no more than
when I had bought it three years earlier, and, very foolishly I
sold it. There is a time when selling a property is a good intention. My reasons at this time, however, were emotional and
very short sighted.

My economic stupidity did not end with the sale of my
house. With the money I received from its sale I bought a nice
duplex. However, I never lived in it and at no time attempted
to rent it out. If I had been filled with faith that as God fed the
birds of the air he would similarly supply my needs, perhaps
there would be something worthy of praise in my behaviour but
such was not the case. It was simply that my girlfriend's house
was far from this duplex I had bought and so I had no desire to
live in it. Nor, I am sure, does this reveal a lovely romantic act
of silliness. Rather, it was simply stupid, and in the end I went
to my lawyer to see if I could walk away from the property,
and when told I could, I stopped paying the mortgage and in
essence threw away thousands of dollars I had invested in the
property. Even empty, if I had continued to pay the mortgage I
would have eventually made money. What can I say?

In 1980 my future wife, her father and I drove a Cadillac that
needed to be delivered to BC across the country to Kamloops

in British Columbia. From there we took a bus, arriving in the Greyhound terminal in Vancouver where we were met by friends who took us to their house in White Rock. After my wife and father in law became employed her mother and the rest of her family travelled by train across the country and rejoined my wife and her father.

We were married in 1982 in the church of St. John the Evangelist, an Anglican church, by the Rev. Don Peel, the missionary from India whom I had met years before when I was a student at Western. A little over two years later our daughter was born, in fact, the day after my birthday. We named her Stephanie SiuPing. The SiuPing was obviously the acknowledgment of her Chinese side while Stephanie was the name of a loved sister who had never been able to have children.

Part way through my wife's pregnancy we bought a seafood restaurant in Cloverdale, approximately half way between Vancouver and White Rock. At that time the little town was dying, as residents tended to shop in nearby and larger, Surrey. It was not uncommon for shops around us to close down, and the only ones that seemed to continue were the drugstore opposite, the hotel, a little up the road and our restaurant, named Traveller's Takeout, and we weren't making a lot of money.

We closed the restaurant the day our daughter was born. In the restaurant, just behind the serving counter, there was a rectangular freezer beside a small counter area constructed with an 8 or 10 inch dip that must have contained a piece of equipment at some time, and then a raised counter for the cash register. This dip area was just large enough to fit an empty TV box that we were given by a store across the street from us. Our daughter "lived" in this box for the first year of her life while we worked around her. In the afternoon I would drive down to Vancouver with her and leave her with my mother in law while I worked in Vancouver.

Even with this extra money we were still not making enough money to give us anything much to live on, and so, in order to save expenses we moved out of our apartment in Vancouver and into the large room above the restaurant that, up till then, had served only as a storage area for the business. Into this we put a bed and a TV and lived there for some months until we sold the restaurant. Obviously we had food, and there was a half bathroom on the restaurant level and fortunately our friends were kind enough to let us use their bathroom for the rest of our ablution needs.

Friday and Saturday were relatively busy days for us and usually we did not bank until later in the weekend. One Sunday while we were working downstairs we did not notice a man go upstairs into our "flat". I had about $700 in one of my suit pockets from the previous day's business. He stole this and slipped out. The police station was nearby and as soon as I discovered that the money was missing I went to the police and told them what had happened. It was too late. The thief had fled and money that could have been used to pay bills was lost, nor was there any way we could prove that we had had the money, or even how much this had been.

Though we were novices in the food industry our fish and chips were quite tasty. This obviously impressed one of our customers, a building contractor. He loved our food and suggested that we go into business together in Kerrisdale, Vancouver, an up market area, the complete opposite of our present location, that promised good business. Serendipitously, the lease was about to run out and we planned to take all our equipment out of the building and use it in the new location. Two events put an end to this delightful plan. First, the customer sadly told us that he could not go into business with us as a much larger contractor who owed him more than a hundred thousand had so far failed to pay him and he had no money for the plan.

However, our lease had indeed run out and we intended to go ahead with the planned move despite our lack of a partner with money. With this in mind, having removed the glass from the front of the store, we were about to try to manipulate a large piece of equipment through the front window when the landlord literally came running in frantically telling us to stop. He no doubt saw his rent money flying out the window along with our equipment. His plan was to get his friend to buy our business. This he eventually did.

We always felt sorry for these people. I have no idea what he told them, and I hope they did better than we did, but we sold the business, paid all our bills and went back to a normal life where other people could pay us and they would have the worry of finding the money. After two years of barely breaking even we actually began to have money in the bank. It was just as well we sold when we did. Our daughter was just beginning to stand up and the TV carton; well it could no longer help.

The next few years were relatively uneventful. On weekends we drove to interesting or beautiful places around Vancouver and in Washington State. Occasionally we took the car ferry across to Vancouver Island to walk around Victoria, the capital, or visit Butchart Gardens. And so, life returned to a less stressful normal and, reflecting on this time, pleasant routine.

Return and Return

In 1989, however, we migrated to Australia so that I could finish my seminary degree. I had never forgotten that I had not completed the degree I began in Toronto, and for a now forgotten reason I applied to St Francis college in Brisbane, my hometown, to rectify this. In North America the degree students studied for was called a Master of Divinity. In Australia, however, the degree sought was a Bachelor of Theology. Having studied for both I am not able to discover any degree of greater or lesser difficulty in either of the degrees, both are post-graduate degrees of a sort.

In my case I suppose I didn't migrate as I had dual citizenship. I had lost my Australian citizenship when I became a Canadian, but years later when I discovered I could get my Australian citizenship back I had very happily done so.

We arrived in Brisbane in August and for several months stayed in my brother's house at the edge of the city while waiting for the school year to begin in January. Sometime close to the start of school, both for me and for our five year old daughter we decided to rent a house near both our schools. Milton State School was just around the corner from our house and St Francis College was at the end of the street, just down from the XXXX brewery at the top of the hill.

One of our daughter's favourite things, apart from a large snail that lived in our aquarium, was a six-inch long mechanical dog that when you wound it up could do somersaults. Somehow this dog became lost and Stephanie was desolate. Our solution to her tears was to drive to the Toowong shopping Mall, our air-conditioned refuge on really hot days, and look for another dog. Fortunately we were able to find an exact copy of her dog, and we returned home with our comforted daughter. A short time later we found the lost dog, and so she ended up with two of her favourite leaping toys.

> *Bending over my daughter,*
> *sleeping,*
> *I ask why it is*
> *I love her.*

The perhaps miraculous finding of lost but valued things occurred one more time after we returned to Canada, momentarily to leap forward a few years. While walking or playing with a friend in Calgary, my daughter lost a small piece of jewelry. I thought the odds of finding the jewelry were extremely small but I went with her to the park and was retracing where she had been when I noticed something sparkling in a tiny stream I reached down and pulled out what she had lost. She was clearly happy, but I think I was more amazed that it had been found. I think it was perhaps an act of the kindness of God.

Holding my daughter's hand
in the dark before sleep,
she had her ears pierced today
thirteen years old,
I realized that
for her to grow up
I must grow older,
that when she is the age
I was
when she was born,
she will probably no longer have
her father
and he will no longer have
his daughter.

I have not been a perfect father, far from it. What I wanted was not to be like my father, and only God knows how much or little I have succeeded in that.

The house on Haig road in Milton was a terrifying surprise for my wife. From the overhanging eaves of the house huge spider webs reached down to the body of the house and in these webs were spiders larger than fifty-cent pieces. The fact that these spiders were not dangerous or poisonous did not reduce my wife's horror. A little work with a broom cleared them off and we went inside to begin our stay in this country that, in contrast to Canada, seems to explode with all kinds of botanical and animal life.

There were cute little three inch lizards about the thickness of a thin drinking straw that scurried around under the grass canopy, and larger, more scary looking blue tongued lizards that preferred that environment as well, but neither of these were dangerous. We could also regularly see a variety of birds; parrots, Blueys and Greenies (though that is not their scientific name, the only difference being that greenies did not have any blue or red colouring) that would descend on the flowering umbrella tree at the front of the house in the spring and brush (or maybe bush) turkeys that appeared in the empty lot behind us. Of course there were also kookaburras, magpies, peewees and other common birds.

Our house, in fact, seemed surrounded by an unplanned collection of trees and shrubs, often filled with various kinds of fruit and flowers and birds. (no poetic atmosphere intended)

How still the air,
from the Jacaranda
the song of a magpie.
Early morning sun.

Early morning,
stillness,
the sound of falling leaves.

Sipping ginger ale
I gaze out the large kitchen windows,
Cool sunlight reflecting off
still
new mango leaves.

On this tiny lot we had Papaya and Banana trees and next-door, open to us as there was no fence dividing us, was a large mulberry tree. I once found a two-inch silky oak seedling growing under our front steps and planted it on the boundary between the two houses. By the time we left it had grown to about fifteen or sixteen feet, straight up like a pine, though many silky oaks have anything but a straight trunk.

Australia is a large continent and the state where we were living ranges from rather sub-tropical in the south around Brisbane, to decidedly tropical in the far north. And yet a winter night-time in Brisbane can feel uncomfortably cold, as many of the older houses do not have any insulation or thermal windows and one must depend on electric heaters to vanquish the cold.

Early each morning, as they had done for perhaps a century, the milkman would travel along our street and drop off two or three bottles of milk on our front steps, indeed on most of the front steps of the houses along the street. Whoever lived in these houses, would leave sufficient coins on the steps to cover the milk and any change would be left with the milk. I discovered that this had been going on for almost a century because under our steps in the dirt I found coins dating from the time of the First World War, pennies and halfpennies, and ten and twenty cent coins from when the new decimal currency of the present began to be used. My brother brought his metal detector to the house to see if I had missed any more coins, but we didn't find much else.

Life began to take on a normal look when my wife was given a job in a new hotel in the downtown opposite the Botanical Gardens and right on the Brisbane River. I was given a job teaching Chinese English teachers how to teach new teachers to teach English. And well done if you can follow that.

I cannot remember that I said anything particularly marvellous at the job interview and I never understood why they gave me this job. I always felt a bit like Woody Allen who said "I wouldn't want to belong to a club that would accept me as a member." This shouldn't be construed as evidence of a lack of self-confidence. I honestly do not think I said anything particularly brilliant at the interview. Nevertheless, the job went well and I believe I fulfilled their expectations. Eventually the program I was in moved from Griffiths University to a campus of the Queensland University of Technology where I taught until we moved back to Canada. I also got a job at TAFE, which is similar to a community college in North America. This was fun and between my wife and me we were able to live and pay the bills.

Though I was a student at an Anglican seminary, we regularly went to a nearby Baptist church. Also attending this church was a Japanese couple with two children. The husband was a graduate student at the University though he was actually a teacher at a university in Idaho in the US. We befriended them, perhaps because we were both outsiders in Australia, and once, during the summer we invited them to go with us to the North Coast to a beach. Our car was an old Holden and among other qualities it possessed was a hole on the front passenger side floor through which the road could be easily seen "racing along under us".

Unknown to us, though we had been using the car for some time, some cockroaches had evidently chosen to make their home in the body of the car. Australian cockroaches are particularly large, two to two and a half inches long. They can also fly. It was a hot day in summer when we went to the beach with our Japanese friends and the heat or the activity of all the people in the car must have disturbed the poor cockroaches, for suddenly about half way to the beach there were cries from the back seat as both parents and children were suddenly invaded by numbers of cockroaches running all around the floor under their feet. We pulled into a gas station and somehow the "problem" was rectified. However, I do not recall ever getting to that beach.

This faded orange Holden with the rather large hole in the floor served us well, taking us north to Rockhampton, where the Great Barrier Reef begins (or ends) and allowing us to get taken to a small island where we were able to view the coral and tropical fish through a glass bottomed boat. On another journey in our less than romantic car, we travelled south to Sydney, then to Canberra and then east to a little town on the coast named, very appropriately my wife and I thought, Eden. We both fell in love with this beach town and hope that someday we can return.

Life was sometimes interesting and disturbing, not only in my car but also where I was studying. In second year, I believe, I enrolled as a part time student in an MA program in religious studies at the University of Queensland. One of my courses at seminary was a study of feminism given by a Catholic nun. One assignment in this course involved an essay for which I was given an A, and the comment that the essay had been quite good. I was enrolled in a similar course at the university, also taught by a Catholic nun who, it turned out, was a friend of the other nun, and I handed in the same essay I had written for the course at seminary. This time I was given a B with the comment that the essay was not particularly insightful. If nothing else, this taught me not to take marks and comments, good or bad, too seriously, that marking is a quite subjective evaluation.

However, just to prove I had not totally learnt this lesson, another marking experience occurred that still leaves me wondering. In a course on Indian religion each student had to present their paper to the class. One of the students, who happened to be a girl, presented her paper to much acclaim and high marks. I could not believe my ears. The paper was truly beautiful as regards form, but, as far as I was concerned, virtually empty of any significant content. She had presented no important ideas nor come to any significant conclusions. At the risk of sounding proud, which I do not believe was actually an issue, I believed, as far as ideas and other content were concerned, that my paper was, if not immeasurably better, then at least significantly so.

I received a lower grade and a day or so after the class went to the American professor, whose area was psychology, to request a re-evaluation of my paper. He gave me a slightly higher grade and then began to tear into me, angrily attacking my personality. Neither then nor now did I understand why he was criticizing me. I could not recognize anything in me that corresponded to his attacks, and I do not think his attack was either appropriate or warranted. However, I did learn that what one believes is reasonable may not be seen as such by others.

Further, given the emotional level of his attack, I cannot but wonder why I, who had had almost no contact with him previously, had disturbed him so deeply. Did he resent the fact that I had questioned his evaluation of my paper? Perhaps it was that he was offended that I thought his evaluation of the girl's presentation was faulty, and I do, though in retrospect I do not recall ever mentioning her paper.

Nevertheless, though I did not and still do not understand this response to the one and only time I ever asked for a re-evaluation of my work, it did not fill my thoughts for long. Life in Australia was, on the whole, a lot of fun. I did with my family what my father had done with us. On many Sundays in the summer we travelled down to the Gold Coast to swim. We even went to the same places.

Rainbow Bay, the last little curve of white sand in Queensland before the state of New South Wales begins, is a beach for families. There is calm water for a little way before the four or five foot waves begin to rise and curl and break over whoever is unlucky enough to be in the wrong place. However, once you learn to get out to where the water rises just before it breaks, and passes over you, you can relax in the warm sub-tropical water as it gently lifts you up and lets you down as you wait for the next wave. I discovered that I loved swimming in the ocean even more than I had as a child.

At least on two occasions, probably during the long Easter weekend, my father rented a house at Rainbow Bay for a family holiday. There is a large rocky outcrop at the right end of the beach, and as children we would explore the rock pools at low tide to see the small fish and anemones that were living in these or trapped there by the receding tide. There were also small octopuses hiding in crevices in the pools and if you pushed a small stick into these crevices, often an octopus would take hold of the stick with its tentacles. I do not remember what we did with these small creatures but I suspect a respect for another creature's life did not possess me at this time.

A little further on, within walking distance from the small house we rented, was a large, relatively flat rocky outcrop called Snapper Rocks, on which two large swimming pool sized pools had been dug. One was, indeed, a swimming pool but the other was a large pool for things like sharks. I do not remember any sharks being in this pool, though there must have been one or two. What I do remember, however, was a fully grown sawfish shark with a long flat extension at the front of its head, maybe two metres long, from which things like teeth grew, with spaces between each "tooth", thus explaining the name of the fish. Waves used to crash on the rocks at the ocean end of these pools.

The two pools were later destroyed and the shark part, which had morphed into a dolphin exhibit was sold to Seaworld a little way up the coast, and both pools broken up, probably for safety reasons as they were, at that point, no longer part of a business and not supervised.

When I was young I would tell anyone who would listen, that until the temperature was 80 degrees the water was too cold to swim in. I probably thought this because that was how we all thought, how we all decided when it was time to go to the beach. We could never understand the tourists who came north from the southern states and swam in what we imagined was freezing water.

However, for them, our winter was summer. It was not that they didn't know what real summer was, but they experienced a much colder winter than we in Queensland could imagine. If you could jump in a plane in the south, travel from Melbourne to Sydney and finally to Brisbane, and check what people are wearing in winter, the further north you go, the less clothing people will be wearing. And if you went to the far north, on a very "cold" day people would be wearing a light sweater, and shorts.

Most people learn to swim in Australia, and the reason is quite simple. Most of the population lives on or near the coast, from Northern Queensland, all the way down and around to

Adelaide in South Australia, and even across to the southern tip of Western Australia. The fact is, Australia is a hot country, seemingly designed, at least for the first two or three hundred kilometres inland, for the comfortable relaxation and pleasure of its inhabitants.

So life continued. My wife continued working, my daughter went to school, just around the corner from our house and in 1992 entered grade four, and I found myself in the last year at seminary and still doing course work at the University of Queensland. There are two kinds of master's degrees: course work master's and thesis master's. I was doing a course work degree. Rightly or wrongly, I always thought a course work degree was not as respectable as a thesis degree and because of this I began finding out about universities in Canada that offered thesis degrees in Religious Studies. Why I settled on the University of Calgary I cannot recall.

I wrote to them telling the department what I had done and what I was doing academically and the department head wrote back saying that I was the kind of person they wanted. In my ignorance I took this as an acceptance of my application and began planning our leave from Australia and all that we were involved with in Australia as individuals and as a family.

To become an Australian citizen one had to live in Australia for three years. I was already a citizen but my wife and daughter were immigrants and by the time we would be returning to Canada they would have been in Australia for almost three years. In fact, as we had arrived around August approximately three years earlier, if we had stayed just a little longer they could have applied for citizenship. This possibility did not enter my head, and I add this to those things I have done and those I have left undone that I carry around with me and about which I have deep regrets.

When I appeared at the Religious Studies Department I am sure they were as disturbed to see me as I was to discover I had not been admitted as a graduate student. After telling them that I had taken my entire family thousands of miles around the globe based on an understanding that they had accepted me, they and the graduate studies department agreed to accept me as an unclassified student who would be taken into the graduate program if I maintained a certain GPA, grade point average, for the coming year.

This I was able to do, so that in the second year we were in Calgary I was finally a graduate student in the Department. For some time I had wanted to do a thesis on Jodo Shinshu, a Japanese form of Buddhism that has interesting similarities to New Testament doctrines on salvation by grace. In Australia I had done at least one Japanese language course at the university and so when I was finally accepted I spoke to the professor who would be my advisor in the field. He was actually a priest in this particular sect, which the majority of Japanese actually belong to.

In the course of my first interview with him he informed me that not only would I need to control modern Japanese but that I would also need Classical Japanese, and it might also be good to be familiar with Classical Chinese. Japanese employs Chinese characters in its writing system and apart from the fact that there are thousands of these employed in multiple combinations, most of the work I would be involved in would be written text. If you have never attempted to learn Chinese or Japanese let me humbly inform you that this is a seriously daunting task.

I am uncertain as to whether I told him that if this were true I would probably end up committing suicide, but I definitely thought it, though certainly not as a serious intent. At the time I was almost fifty years old and I did not think I had the time to go down that particular road to insanity and still have time for a career. I changed advisors, and naturally with this, my thesis topic.

Sometime in our stay in Calgary my daughter, who was at this time in grade four or five, and I drove to Prince Edward

Island with the sole purpose of visiting the land of Anne of Green Gables. I had read virtually all the Anne books, one chapter at a time, to her before she went to sleep and "Anne" had become an important "person". At the time we had a small Toyota Tercel, and with this we set out on our journey east. Having driven easily though the remainder of Alberta, Saskatchewan and Manitoba along straight well paved highways we struggled through the narrow windy Ontario section of the Trans Canada.

Somewhere in moose country we just avoided a collision with one of these very large beasts, which would have put a speedy end to our trip, our car and probably our lives as it crashed down onto the car crushing all concerned. These animals seem to be mostly legs and hitting one would have been like knocking down skittles, that is until the hundreds of pounds above the legs rapidly began to descend on the car.

We arrived safely in London, Ontario where my sister lived and took the pleasantly unavoidable day trip to Niagara Falls, which never fails to impress. In one of the busy intersections of the town my gear stick suddenly completely fell apart and I have no idea how we eventually got through the intersection. If I remember correctly, my daughter tells me she had decided to unscrew the top of the gear stick and at this opportune moment it chose to come apart, sending all the different little bits, in a manner of speaking, "into the air". Having reassembled the gear shift we finished with Niagara Falls and returned to London, not at all sure we had a car that would guarantee that small distance. And London, if we went no further, was only half the journey.

My sister and two of her children took over at this point, and we travelled the rest of the pilgrimage in her car whose only mechanical problem seemed to be that occasionally the door locks would refuse to function and the doors would not stay shut. We travelled through the rest of Ontario, and into beautiful Quebec and, forgive me, boring New Brunswick (all forest and few people until you reach the coast). After driving across the twelve kilometer Confederation Bridge we found a place to rest our heads in PEI and began to look around. I am sure we ate fish and chips, and for a few moments, paid our respects at the grave of Lucy Maud Montgomery, the author of the Anne books, my daughter and I putting two or three wild flowers on her grave. As might be expected, we went through the Anne of Green Gables house and walked through its nearby woods. This had been the reason for the trip.

We loved Prince Edward Island. It is green and beautiful, small enough to drive around easily and obviously surrounded by ocean. A short time later we bought two side by side quarter acre lots near Tracadie Bay. However, we discovered we would have had to make a small road to get to this property and it was heavily treed. Fortunately, we were able to exchange these two lots for 1.3 acres, roughly in the middle of the Island and on the corner of a paved road and Sheepskin Lane, a red dirt side road that leads down through over-arching trees to a huge corn field at the lower edge of the property. We love this little bit of the Island and have, over the years attempted to thin out the small young trees that block the view from the road, but so far have never built on it. We are on one side of a very large country, and it is on the completely opposite side, thousands of kilometers away. A truly fascinating problem.

Years later, in 2019, I flew out to Prince Edward Island to see if we could live on our land during the winter, in the course of which I met an architect I had been e-mailing to ask about building plans I had. Her comments did not encourage me. I wanted to build a house with a traditional Chinese roof, and dig a small lake beside which would be a Chinese teahouse, open but with a Chinese roof. I wanted the house to be dug into the ground for the purpose of insulation, so that only the kitchen and living and dining rooms would be above ground. Below would be a large Perspex window that opened onto the lake so that fish could be seen from the room below ground. It would have cost more money than I thought I could raise, even from the sale of a house on Vancouver Island.

Later, from other people I spoke to, I realized that at our age it would also be quite difficult to live in PEI during the winter. We have lived through many Alberta winters, but PEI winters can be even more extreme.

Before I returned to the West I began discussions with the neighbour who owned the 1.3 acre lot next to ours, to find out if he was interested in buying our land. Happily, he was, and we eventually sold the land my family loved. If the winters were not so severe, I am fairly certain we would have eventually built on the land and moved there. I had such dreams for this place; they were not to be.

We ended up living in Calgary for almost eleven years and several times during this stay we drove east so I could visit my family and friends in London. Our car was not air-conditioned and we certainly did not have much money so we wound down the windows to get cooler air (a rather futile attempt) and slept in the car to save money. We usually stopped for breaks and food at the same places. These became pleasantly familiar stops... a little 'chain' restaurant in Medicine Hat, and further on, at a very simple restaurant on a relatively deserted stretch of Highway 1 at the top of Lake Superior.

Sometime in these eleven years I travelled to Abraham Lincoln's tomb in Springfield, once by myself and the second time with my wife. The first time I had no idea what I was going to, but it was mainly respect for a great president and person. The second visit was to express respect a final time, not for just one of the greatest presidents but also for one who was able to forgive enemies and work with them.

I usually drove about 8 or 900 kilometres a day but one night after I had been driving all day, I must have been driving at about 20 kilometres an hour and a police car stopped me to find out if I was drunk. I don't think I realized how slow I was driving, but after deciding I did not seem to be dangerously intoxicated, he told me I should stop as soon as I could find a place and sleep. I thought this was good advice and obeyed.

Despite all the inconvenience and summer heat, the drives across Canada with my wife and daughter were beautiful discoveries of a beautiful country. Later, when we had better cars, air-conditioning and slightly more money we stayed in motels, or flew, but the earlier journeys, almost because of their lack of comfort, gave us, I think, richer memories.

Calgary is a relatively short drive into the Rocky Mountains and the drive is almost continually a beautiful display of field and river framed by dolomite mountain ranges. We often stopped, just outside Canmore (another of our favourite places) in a very small provincial park and had a barbecue picnic beside the Bow river that flowed quickly past. On another picnic we had just finished, had packed the car and were just leaving when we saw a black bear ambling up the road about a hundred yards from where we had just had the picnic. We stopped to look at the bear (from inside the car) when five or ten cyclists who were climbing the steep road anxiously told us to move. I suspect they were in more danger if we actually did so, unless, of course, they simply were tired of tourists stopping to "annoy" the wildlife.

I eventually got the degree, in the process completing twice as many courses as required for both the Religious Studies degree I completed in Calgary and the theology courses from Wycliffe and the ones I studied at St Francis College in Australia to finally complete the theology degree. (Oddly, the transcript Wycliffe sent to St Francis College in Australia was not a transcript of my courses. So I was admitted to St Francis based on someone else's courses and marks. I did not attempt to correct this mistake.) Does this say anything about my organizational skills? Both degrees were certainly not the normal paths to a career, but I think any failure on my part can only be in relation to the M.A. It was my decision to change schools and start another degree in Canada.

On the other hand, though I really could not have finished the M.Div. in Toronto because of intellectual conflicts concerning the problem of suffering, was there a relationship between this issue and my overall personality? Don't normal people simply start, do the required course work acquire the expected degree and continue on to a career based on their education? Yet, one cannot be other than what one is, and hopefully that results in a positive, creative end.

Moving from the University of Queensland to Calgary so that I could do a thesis degree rather than a course MA is a different issue. I have always thought that a thesis is a more serious academic work than simply completing a number of courses. So was it pride that caused me to leave Australia and return to Canada? Couldn't I have waited till my daughter finished her year at school? How thoughtless was my decision to uproot the family one more time? This is not a rhetorical question.

The older I grow the more I become aware of the suffering I have, or may have caused other people as a result of the many, many decisions I have made in my journey through life. How many have been harmed because of behaviours and ideas that, at the time, I thought were perfectly acceptable? One cannot, after all, go back and correct one's life mistakes.

Further, I believe I have not done justice to my father. Hatred refuses to see the good in other people and at the time I was incapable of seeing any in him. I do not now believe he hated me. Perhaps he was just unable to love sufficiently. Also, one's own suffering always causes one to lash out at those closest, and this usually means one's family, and I now realize that this could apply to me as it does to my father. Not only does one need God's forgiveness, one also needs the forgiveness of one's fellow human beings, and frequently, one's family.

Since I received my degree I have done several things that could be seen as eminently praiseworthy and unusual, and

others of an opposite nature. There was a time several years
back, when I thought, "I have travelled to many places around
the world, though not all that I would like, and I have achieved
enough to give me the faith that my life has not been wasted".
I no longer feel this way. I am dependent each day on the help,
encouragement and strength of God, and for this I am grateful,
as King David said, "well though he knows me".

*If I were born
a thousand times
I'm sure
not all those years to learn
would lighten my dark soul
What ever have I learnt
that went so deep
that it could stop
a sinful heart
that knows
but does not do.
The old word does the job.
It is,
and I
a Franciscan beggar
naked, poor and unacceptably weak
painfully aware
of what I really am,
tremblingly take for myself
the Good Man's robe.*

Meditation 1

A Meditation on David, King of Israel

A Biblical View of the Sinner
2 Samuel 11-12,14 & 2 Samuel 7:20

M ost serious Christians know, or at least believe, that psalm 51, the penitential psalm, was written by David after he sinned with Bathsheba. They know this, but rarely do they ever think about it. They may speak about his sin, but they do not think about it, and this is so, generally speaking, because they are so dominated by, in thrall to the idea of David as the friend of God, as the King of Israel, the composer of Psalms, the one chosen by God over Saul who *one time* went into battle without seeking God's guidance and blessing. They are so suffused with those images that his sin, the reason for Psalm 51, is diminished, made small and taken lightly, ever so lightly, almost of no account, in comparison.

They think of David as a holy man, the one who passionately sought the return of the Ark and rejoiced with dancing at its return, the one who knew God from his youth, who slew Goliath with a stone from his slingshot. They do not care to think of him as the rapist who violated Bathsheba, as an adulterer, the murderer of Uriah and the deceiver who sought to cover up this adultery with murder in order to escape its consequences. This they do not think about.

But what did Joab, David's general and co- conspirator in the murder think after the event? Do you think he ever looked at David and thought, "I know you, you hypocrite, you criminal. You write your delightful psalms but I know what you did!" David had instructed Joab to go close to the wall of a city they were besieging and then pull back, leaving Uriah to face possible, and almost certain death. Joab's instructions to the messenger to David were that if David became angry at this he was to say, "And Uriah your servant was also killed." Oh, how beautiful, how the sarcasm, the insult, the ridicule of David fills this little sentence. "Your servant Uriah". It was not simply, "And Uriah is dead". "Your servant is dead."

David had rewarded Uriah's deep loyalty by having him killed and attempting to make his death appear accidental. Joab knew what he was saying. And he also knew that David could say and do nothing about the implied accusation and ridicule in the comment. Perhaps he realized that the king was not to be trusted, despite even deep loyalty to David. Moreover, Joab, at the end of David's life, chose to ally himself with Adonijah who set himself up as king without consulting David. This suggests that while Joab continued to have power in David's court he did not have a close relationship with the king and may have sought occasion to undermine David's prerogatives.

What was, in fact, the nature of Bathsheba's marriage to Uriah? Uriah was a Hittite, not a Jew. Had the marriage been arranged, or was it, at least to some degree, a marriage of love? The narrator appears completely uninterested in the social dynamics of Bathsheba's marriage and never hints at her feelings or reactions to both David's intercourse with her and the death of her husband. We are never told how she reacted to Uriah's death. The only thing of importance is David's behaviour and the only emotion suggested in the narrative is his sexual desire.

Did the narrator ever attempt to learn what Bathsheba felt? The story's silence suggests that women were very low in the hierarchy of power in Israel, as indeed they have traditionally been in almost every culture. This lack of power does, however, indicate that resistance to David's passion by Bathsheba would have been virtually impossible.

When David first saw Bathsheba as she was bathing, he was on the roof of his palace. But think for a moment. They did not have binoculars or telescopes in those days. He could not see the details of her body; the visual sensation of her body near him would have been lacking. What he saw, at best, was a moving naked body that allowed the idea of sensuality *and that is all*. And, unless she stopped and turned to face him so that he had the time to examine her, which seems unlikely, the terrible events that followed from this moment resulted from an almost certainly brief and incomplete glimpse of Bathsheba.

Did he later order her to be invited to the palace so that he could see her more closely, see the shape of her body more exactly? After all, it was her body that had attracted him to her, definitely not her mind or personality. Perhaps he had seen her before, on the street or maybe even in his palace and had been attracted to her. Maybe he had wanted her sexually even before he saw her naked on the roof of her house.

And in this unreal situation, did Bathsheba feel she had the power, the right to refuse the king when he told her he wanted to have sex with her? Did he even ask her? Could anyone, especially a woman, refuse the king? Or, do we imagine she was some kind of mindless robot who was not conscious that what was happening was not only a violation of the Law of God but a breaking of a powerful social taboo that could have terrible consequences, especially for a woman?

In later years, did she ever look at David and remember being raped by him? Is there another word for what he did? Did she look at him, and in that look say, "I remember what happened. You may fool your people but I know what you are, you hypocrite!" Or had she forgiven him?

Did Nathan, the prophet, the man of righteousness, the moral man, the man who finally confronted David, during the ensuing years, see David as a man of God or only as a murderer and adulterer? Did Nathan remember David's sin every time he saw him from then on, or did he take the forgiveness of God seriously? Or did Nathan do what we often attempt to do? Admit God's forgiveness but continue to nurture our own unforgiving attitude, murmuring in our hearts, "God may have forgiven you, but you are still an evil man." Was it that Nathan, the righteous prophet could only view David in a single light, as a murderer and adulterer?

Nathan's loyalty to David at the end of David's life suggests otherwise, that Nathan had, in fact, accepted that God had forgiven David and saw David as a changed repentant man. Does this perhaps raise the question of how we should view a repentant forgiven sinner? Indeed, which of all these various views of David reveals the attitude of God?

What, in fact, did David think of himself? Did he write the psalm and then forget about the whole horrible experience? Personally, I do not think he was ever able to forget what he had done. I imagine that many times when he saw Bathsheba he remembered. I imagine he thought that after he had raped her and killed Uriah, taking her as his wife was the only thing he could do.

But let us pause. Perhaps the truth was quite different. Perhaps Bathsheba was bathing on her roof to "tell" David he could have her. Perhaps she was already aware that he wanted her. Perhaps her marriage to Uriah was not a happy one and she saw a way to entrap David. Later, could it also have been that Bathsheba was angry at Uriah for his ridiculous display of loyalty to David in choosing not to come home to her when he reported to David, staying the night at the gate of the palace, and consequently *not* giving *her* an excuse for her pregnancy? Why should we assume that David was the only guilty one?

Yet David is really the issue. The issue is the godly king who murdered and had sex with the married Bathsheba. Moreover, none of the possibilities in this previous paragraph may be true, they are not suggested in the tale, whereas the details supplied in the narrative possess reasonable implications. In addition, for David to promise that Solomon would be his heir suggests that the king did not feel that he had been entrapped. A strong case against Bathsheba seems unlikely.

Moreover, in 1 Kings 1:13 we find the words, "Did not your majesty swear to me, your servant, that my son Solomon should succeed you as king?" And later, verse 30 reads, "I swore by the Lord, the God of Israel, that Solomon your son should succeed me." Does this not indicate the depth of wrongdoing he felt towards Bathsheba that he would promise that her son Solomon would follow him as king? Not only did David reiterate what he had promised, but named Solomon as "your son". There was a close connection to Bathsheba in David's promise, and I would suggest, an open acknowledgement of the great guilt that had led up to Bathsheba's marriage to David.

I imagine that often, as he lay on his bed before he went to sleep, he remembered what he had done with horror and shame, remembered that he had used deceit, lies to attempt to cover up his crime. I imagine, even after he knew God had forgiven him, that he remembered all these things, often, and unhappily.

When God promised that his kingly line would be lasting, David was obviously and deeply thankful, but David added at the end of his prayer to God, "Well though thou knowest me." It was not simply that *God* knew what kind of person he was. David also knew. The words could as easily be said as, "Well though I know myself!" Was David ever able, after all this, to be the spiritual man he had previously been? Did he have the confidence to speak of God before people who silently knew what he had done? Could he ever again be a spiritual authority after all this?

Wherever David looked after the event he saw eyes that knew. When he looked at those, perhaps closest to him, he knew that they knew, and almost certainly, he sometimes wondered what they thought of him.

He had not committed simple little sins, you know the kind, if we are truly honest with ourselves, we imagine we have done, we decent people who can look others in the eye without shame and fear. We know we have not committed any really terrible sins. We do not have a scarlet letter burned into our being for others to see. David, on the other hand, knew he had committed huge sins and he would have to live with the memory of them for the rest of his life, even after, and with the assurance of the forgiveness of God. God, you see, was not his problem. We were. So I ask, "What do you think of David?"

Meditation 2

S ince writing this I have come to understand, at least one of the weaknesses of the meditation. I wrote the meditation so that people would take the horror of David's sins seriously, and in doing this, hopefully transfer their willingness to "see" but "forgive" David, to a similar willingness to see but forgive contemporary people guilty of similarly terrible behaviours.

However, I strongly suspect that people of today do not conceive of David's sins with any deep sense of their reality. For today's readers it is a too familiar, and yet unfamiliar story, the details of which do not resonate with any contemporary acts of horror and repulsion. People see David's sins/crimes simply as a story. That is, it doesn't strike them as behaviours of an actual person in real time.

In an attempt to counter the unreality of the biblical story let me hypothesize that within one's circle of acquaintances and friends there is a horrendous genocidal killer. Let me ask, in that situation, what one's attitude to the killer would be, if that person was not repentant? Now let me add another variable. What would one's attitude to this person be if this person was repentant, and you, as a friend or acquaintance, were convinced that they were sincerely repentant?

In response to the horror of the deeds would you continue to feel repulsion towards the person, despite his repentance, or would you feel an acceptance of the person based upon the fact that God had forgiven this individual his terrible behaviour?

There is no question that a sense of horror towards the nature of the evil deeds is justified. How could one feel otherwise? What I would like to focus on is the nature of one's attitude towards the individual, guilty of such horrendous acts.

Do we respond as Christians to one who has been forgiven, or do we continue to act as an unbeliever would, who seeks only the punishment and social exclusion of the offender? Do we respond as Christians, or do we respond as pagans?

Tell me why a Christian could wish an offender to be punished, if there had been repentance and the acts have been forgiven by God. What would the purpose of the punishment, that you so fervently wish, be? And if you continue to believe the offender should still, nevertheless, be punished, how do you view your own sins? Despite having been forgiven by God, should not God also punish you as you wish this "other sinner" to be punished? And, in fact, were not your sins to result in an eternity in hell?

Quite frankly, you either accept Matthew 7:3-5, Luke 7:36-50, Luke 15:11-32, and Matthew 18:23-35, and take these seriously, or you don't. There is no middle ground.

CPSIA information can be obtained
at www.ICGtesting.com
Printed in the USA
BVHW042339221020
591453BV00026BA/230